WITHDRAWN

THE SACRED GEOGRAPHY OF THE AMERICAN MOUND BUILDERS

(THE SACRED GEOGRAPHY OF THE AMERICAN MOUND BUILDERS)

Maureen Korp

Native American Studies
Volume 2

The Edwin Mellen Press
Lewiston/Queenston/Lampeter

Library of Congress Cataloging-in-Publication Data

Korp, Maureen.
   The sacred geography of the American mound builders / by Maureen
Korp.
      p. cm. -- (Native American studies ; v. 2)
   Includes bibliographical references (p.).
   ISBN 0-88946-484-7
   1. Mound builders. 2. Adena culture. 3. Hopewell culture.
4. Mississippian culture. 5. Mounds--North America. 6. Indians of
North America--Religion. 7. Indians of North America--Antiquities.
I. Title. II. Series.
E73.K67 1990
974'.01--dc20
                                                          89-28543
                                                              CIP

This is volume 2 in the continuing series
Native American Studies
Volume 2 ISBN 0-88946-484-7
NAS Series ISBN 0-88946-482-0

A CIP catalog record for this book
is available from the British Library.

The Edwin Mellen Press   The Edwin Mellen Press
        Box 450   Box 67
   Lewiston, New York   Queenston, Ontario
     USA 14092   CANADA, L0S 1L0

              The Edwin Mellen Press, Ltd.
                 Lampeter, Dyfed, Wales
              UNITED KINGDOM SA48 7DY

            Printed in the United States of America

To the peoples of the "poorly known tribes"

CONTENTS

vi

LIST OF ILLUSTRATIONS

Figure

Illustration Credits

Donna Silver, figs. 1, 2, 5, 8, 9, 13, 16, 27, and 28; John A. Eddy, "Medicine Wheels and Plains Indian Astronomy" from *Native American Astronomy*, edited by Anthony F. Aveni, ©1975 by University of Texas Press, figs. 3 and 4; Florida State Archives, fig. 6; Jon L. Gibson, *Poverty Point*, ©1985 by Louisiana Archaeological and Antiquities Commission, fig. 7; Marija Gimbutas, *The Gods and Goddesses of Old Europe, 7000 to 3500 BC*, ©1974 by Thames and Hudson, fig. 9; William N. Morgan *Prehistoric Architecture in the Eastern United States*, The MIT Press, figs. 10, 15, 17, 18, 19, 20, 21, 22, 23, 24, 25, and 26; E. G. Squier and E. H. Davis, *Ancient Monuments of the Mississippi Valley, Smithsonian Contributions To Knowledge, vol. 1,* figs. 11 and 12; David I. Bushnell, Jr., *Natwe Cemeteries and Forms of Burial East of the Mississippi*, Smithsonian Institute, fig. 14.

Acknowledgements

My study began originally as a year-long directed readings project under the supervision of Ruth Phillips, Ph.D., of the Canadian Studies Institute, Carleton University. The bibliographical problems served as a threshing topic for the religious studies graduate seminar, directed by Robert Choquette, Ph.D., University of Ottawa. I am grateful for the assistance and clear direction both have given me as I worked my way through the material. Dr. Phillips was candid in forewarning me that the topic was difficult, but exciting — and she was right. Dr. Choquette, my advisor, rescued the argument more than one time when I tangled it in my hesitation to say what I really meant. Whatever false starts and tangles remain are, of course, my own doing.

I also want to acknowledge the friendly help and interest of persons I know only by telephone and letter in the United States. Many responded to my personal plea for pictorial information. All were generous with their time. They are: Patricia Essenpreis, Ph.D., Department of Anthropology, University of Florida; Nancy Hawkins, Staff Archaeologist, State of Louisiana Office of Cultural Historic Preservation; Linda W. Joslin, Special Projects Coordinator, Arkansas Historic Preservation Program; Joan Morris, Archivist, Florida State Archives; Martha Otto, Ph.D., Curator of Archaeology, Ohio Historical Society; Martha Rolingson, Ph.D., Toltec Mounds State Park, Arkansas; and John Scarry, Ph.D., Archaeological Research Section, Florida Department of State.

Colleagues and friends, too, in Ottawa and New York City proved an invaluable resource. As each became interested in my study, each helped me keep my interest steady. Their telephone calls, letters, and the items they pulled from their bookshelves were always heartwarming, and very often relevant. Those people include: Diane Bridges; Constance Brook; Ronnie Brown; Michael Davidson; Paula Drewek; Margaret Dyment; Evelyn Lee; Patricia Robinson; Donna Silver; Vasanthi Srinavasan; Meryl

Taradash; Dorothy Warnock; Frank White; Helga Wintal; and Dwight Yachuk.

Traditionally the last note of an acknowledgement names the person who kept the household running so the writer could write. I have an especially dear acknowledgement to make here—my daughter, Meghan Taylor Dunn.

My research was supported by a University of Ottawa Graduate Research Scholarship and a departmental assistantship.

FOREWORD

The great expansive landscapes of the broad mid-section of the United States seem sparsely populated. Here and there are farms and small towns, only occasionally a city of any significance. The openness, the vastness of the land, not to mention the formative imagery of United States history with its westward expansion, suggest that the present inhabitants are the first; the first of any significance anyway. The Indians? They were among the wild things displaced by settlement. Yet just below the surface of the land, indeed even as mounded obtrusions in the landscape, is evidence of ancient dramas whose plots can now only be imagined. High dramas they were. The unearthed evidence tell stories in bones, countless bones, human bones. The labor of flesh-and-blood peoples it took to construct the mounds is of such a measure as to astound even us — the peoples of modern earth-moving technologies.

Many of the peoples who lived in ancient times in the huge expanse of the Mississippi River Valley and the valleys of its tributaries buried at least some of their dead in human-constructed mounds. Thousands of these mounds were simple structures, but some reached the enormous proportions of those at Cahokia near present-day East St. Louis. The largest mound there, called Monks Mound, is as tall as a ten-story building and has a mass larger than the Pyramid of Khufu in Egypt. Within a related mound (in which there are more than 250 burials) is the burial of a figure placed face down upon what was apparently a cape or blanket decorated with 10,000 mussel and conch shell beads. This figure is surrounded by three male and three female youths, ages 17 to 21, all buried at the same time, all with heads pointed in the direction of Monks Mound.

These thousands of mounds dotting the landscape attesting to the powerful presence of ancient Americans are rather like a giant page of braille, now damaged by plow and progress, whose code there is not even the hope of ever fully deciphering. Yet, some of the marks, some of the signs, are so potent they whisper still of ancient meanings. Their magnitude, their number, their implications of order attest that they were built with a corresponding measure of intent and significance. Surveys of the many marks upon this bumpy page yield tantalizing correspondences and possibilities. Abducted by the stimulation to the imagination, this cipher must be attended to despite the inevitable failure of ever fully knowing the story behind these impressions.

Maureen Korp presents the drama and the possibilities of these burial sites with clarity and enthusiasm. They come to life for us through her words (complemented by many fine illustrations) and as the result of her painstaking research. Though enthusiastic about the possible meanings of these burials, she is careful never to overstep what can be clearly grounded in the physical evidence. She even reins in some of those who have let their imaginations overtax the evidence.

The physical evidence attests undeniably to the intentionality, the purposiveness of the actions of these ancient peoples. There are suggestions of system and order everywhere. But what was the system? What gave meaning to these actions? What beliefs were being expressed? Ms. Korp focuses upon the directional orientation of the mounds and the burials within the mounds. Her study of the physical evidence demonstrates that special significance was attributed to easterly directionality. But how to provide some content, some elaboration of the meaning of this favored orientation? Ms. Korp turns to the ethnographic record of the mythology and the burial customs of those modern tribal peoples most likely to be the descendants of the ancient mound-builders.

Through careful correlation of materials Ms. Korp constructs what seems likely to have been the broad belief systems which underlay and were being expressed and enacted in the mound-building and burial practices. Her study is an imaginative, yet carefully documented effort to listen to the voices from the ancient past.

Sam D. Gill
Professor, University of Colorado

Chapter I

INTRODUCTION

The Mississippi River, the longest river in North America, begins its southward journey in the far reaches of Minnesota at Lake Itasca. As it rolls forward to the Gulf Coast and the spreading fingers of Louisiana's vast, rich delta land, its major tributaries — the Missouri from the west and the Ohio from the east — join it halfway along. This part of the United States is one better known to tourists for the legendary exploits of Daniel Boone, Joliet and Marquette, and Mark Twain than for those of their precursors — the "mysterious mound builders" — of whom almost nothing is known. In fact, the map which serves as the frontispiece of volume 15, *The Northeast*, of the Smithsonian Institution's *Handbook of North American Indians* identifies this part of the Mississippi River and its tributaries as the land of the "poorly known tribes."

The Paleo-Indian

There have been people here for a very long time, people who followed the Mississippi's tributaries westward across the continent and north and south along the great river itself. The Missouri River, longest of the Mississippi's tributaries, has its origins in the foothills of the Rockies. For the most part, the Missouri takes a wide, slow, meandering course to the Mississippi. The Ohio, however, can be a water gusher. Its valley is narrow, it floods, but it is navigable (See fig. 1).

The earliest of wanderers along these rivers were probably hard-scrabble followers of big game trails, the paleo-Indian (sometimes called, too, the Big Game Hunters or Intermontane peoples). From Siberia they crossed the ice bridging the Bering Strait to the Alaskan mainland in one or many waves,[1] perhaps as long ago as 40,000 BCE, then again as recently as 6,500 to 4,000 years ago.

The hunters had fire and stone tools. They foraged and killed animals, small and large, including the mammoth, mastodon, and elk. They lived not in caves, but on hills and rises of land, in brush windbreaks, perhaps burrowing into earth lodges[2] in the winter. Water was never far away, and they could see the movement of the great herds below. They left evidence of their wanderings—fire hearths, projectile points. Some hearths are dated as far back as 36,000 BCE; however, these findings have not been widely accepted[3] because no other evidence, such as projectile points or human remains, has been found in the same vicinity. One would expect domestic hearths to be more cluttered. On the other hand, Joseph Campbell points out that the presence of a hearth "...may also mean a shrine, or the fire itself a living divinity."[4] Similar hearths in Europe and Asia have been dated as far back as 750,000 BCE in France and 500,000 BCE in China, or the time period of *Homo erectus*. Are the North American fire hearths ones deliberately constructed, or ones accidentally made by lightning? We just do not know.

None of the known or suspected paleo-Indian sites would have been, in any case, permanent settlements. More likely they were no more than mean hunting camps inhabited by small bands of wandering people.

Presumably paleo-Indian hunting campsites are found throughout North America. They are recognized by the presence of stone circles, or tepee rings, and date from early prehistory well into historic times. Tepee rings are circles of stone used to batten down tepees; hence, once gathered, they mark a site for reuse by other visitors to the site. Tepee rings are found scattered all over, from Texas to northern Canada. They number in the millions.[5]

Medicine Wheels

Much more interesting are the large stone rings with radiating spokes usually called "medicine wheels." They can measure as much as 100m in diameter. At the center is often found a stone cairn sometimes 10m wide,[6] sometimes serving as a burial mound.[7] Some of these are the earliest burial sites we know of in North America. Medicine wheels are almost always constructed on elevated sites and command a clear view. The rings and cairns have been dated to as recently as the last century and as long ago as 10,000 years.[8]   Plains and prairie people have long regarded them as sacred, but for reasons they no longer remember.   Some elders think the wheels have something to do with the sun dance; others think they were used by "calendar men," shamans, for who-knows-what purpose.[9]

Big Horn Medicine Wheel is the best known of the sites (see fig. 2). It is in Montana and located in a United States national park.   John Eddy dates Big Horn to 2,500 BCE and presents a persuasive case for its being a calendar marking the summer solstice.   Eddy also thinks the wheel points out the position of three stars, Aldebaran, Rigel, and Sirius, but he is far less persuasive here, calling them "stars of the summer dawn."[10]   He does not explain why they might have such importance to the builders of the wheel, nor do I know of any particular reason from myth or tradition, either.   Other efforts to confirm Aldebaran, Rigel, and Sirius alignments at other sites have failed.[11]

For our purposes what seems to be more important is that Big Horn Medicine Wheel has a pointer (see fig. 3) for everyday east, and that the 28 spokes of the wheel count out a lunar cycle. There is a similar wheel with 28 spokes (it is badly marred) in south-central Alberta known as the Majorville Cairn.   That cairn may date as far back as 7,000 BCE.[12]   It contains more than 45 tonnes of rock.   In other sites Eddy surveyed throughout the Rockies, he notes that mostly the spokes do not point anywhere to cardinal points. What they do is exhibit an easterly preference generally.[13]   If the spokes are pointing to where the sun rises, and to nothing more particular than that – a possibility Eddy omits – that would account for the easterliness of the spokes (see fig. 4) and the lack of a clear cardinal direction in his graphing.

Sunwise, east, is the sacred direction pre-eminently and consistently today in Amerindian religious ritual.   Was east pre-eminent in Amerindian religious ritual long ago?   Even so long ago as the paleo-Indian?

Study Parameters

The question is worth asking even if the only indication the answer is "yes" is the medicine wheel pointer. We know some of the paleo-Indians became in Archaic times Woodland peoples, some became Pueblo, some remained big game hunters on the prairie, and some became mound builders.   In every instance save one we can find in historic times evidence of a concern for east as a sacred direction equivalent to the rising sun.   We cannot for the mound builders. By the start of the European contact period (1492, Columbus' "discovery" of America), all but the last survivors of the Mississippian cultures were gone. For many years those survivors, ravaged in Hernando de Soto's c.1539 coastal explorations of the Gulf Coast and the lower Mississippi Valley, were thought of as a poor provincial footnote to the elegant, impressive, powerful Mesoamerican civilizations further south. The question of Mesoamerican influence in the three mound-building cultures (Adena, Hopewell, Mississippian) is a matter of active investigation and reassessment by scholars today. No consensus has emerged. There are even a few scholars who think the Mississippian platform mounds might have been an indigenous development with only a very late overlay of Mesoamerican influence. It is generally accepted, however, that the descendants of the mound builders are the Woodlands and Plains peoples. The problem is that no one knows who of the Woodlands and Plains were once Adena, Hopewell, or Mississippian. Nevertheless with that much to go on, it is possible to establish useful study parameters. Three have guided my study of sacred directionality in selected Mississippi Valley burial mounds.

First, when considering data from the historic period, I searched only material from the Woodlands people and from Plains people who were formerly Woodlands. Secondly, because the mounds were used earliest as burial sites and possibly as astronomical sites, I considered only similar corresponding practices of burial and sky-gazing from the historic period tribes. I was not concerned with rites of passage, or the role of women, or kinship lines, or any of the other things that occupy the attention of anthropologists except in so far as these pertain to burial ritual or sky-gazing. I presumed burial ritual to be a sacred rite, little given to change or innovation, unless the religious rationale for it changes. Lastly, however attractive it might have been to consider the mound as feminine archetype, as "mother earth," I put this query aside in favour of a clear dead reckoning on sacred directionality. In other words, my concern has been only to demonstrate that east is the rising sun, and that it was a necessary component of an earth interment for the "mysterious mound builders."

Summary of Findings

A description of Poverty Point, a monumental earthwork of the Mississippi delta from the Archaic period, is presented first. This is followed by a simplified outline of the Adena, Hopewell, and Mississippian mound-building cultures (the reader will find the time line, fig. 5, helpful in managing the data of this section). Several burial site orientation factors are discussed. My review of William N. Morgan's survey drawings, published in 1980, certainly suggests that east is consistently the pre-eminent direction and a proximity to water the most important siting factor. E. G. Squier's earlier survey drawings published in 1846, also supports this observation of east as pre-eminent. The next chapter sketches briefly a number of creation myths and historic ritual practices, including burial rites, of the Woodlands and Plains peoples. There is a similar concern for an easterly directional emphasis. The concluding chapter draws attention to important linguistic evidence from the work of Cecil H. Brown for the pre-eminence of east in language directional elements worldwide. Not all archaic languages have four cardinal directional terms, certainly not North American native languages, but all have a word for east, even if some omit a word for north. Brown posits the sequence of entry *into any language* of directional terms to be as follows: first east, then west; then up and down; then south; and sometimes north. East is almost always a word equivalent to or meaning the "rising sun."

Our contemporary emphasis on north—be it polar north or magnetic north—derives from a sailor's need to stay on course at night and a mapmaker's convention of placing north at the top of the page. The sacred directionality of the pre-contact Amerindian is not one based on European navigational method nor need. The ancient Amerindian was not an ocean-voyaging sailor. Even the Northwest Coast people stayed close in to shore, following the channel of the barrier islands. The ancient hunter-gatherer and the ancient planter of North America were not peoples abroad at night. For such people then, what was wanted was a daytime orientation factor. What better direction than east, the direction of the rising sun, the start of the new day. Our usual Western notions of four-square, cardinal directional notation simply do not pertain.

Scholarly and Popular Interest Contrasted

I know of no studies on directionality as a religious motif in Amerindian scholarship. When directional considerations are mentioned, they are only as descriptors of the action taking place. Thus, one reads: "participants moved sunwise," or "entering from the east," or "facing the morning sun." The reader is almost never told why it matters. To date, archaeoastronomy, one of the newest approaches in archaeology, has produced only a handful of studies of the ancient Amerindian sites. Some have considered effigy mounds as solar templates,[14] others have looked for evidence of comet depictions or novas in western rock etchings.[15] There are a few solstice studies of the mounds in Arkansas, Louisiana, Ohio, and Illinois now underway. In 1987, P. Clay Sherrod and Martha Ann Rolingson published their study demonstrating the solstice alignments of the Toltec Mound site near Little Rock, Arkansas.[16] These are all a welcome corrective for the previous inattention paid to cognitive aspects of site orientation in any ancient site. Solstice studies, however, are difficult to do, time-consuming, and — for some reason — their findings almost always provoke controversy rather than applause. The mound builders remain mysterious. Part of the reason for their mystery rests with the bibliography available.

The bibliography[17] is extensive, scattered, and a difficult one with which to work. The archaeological writing tends to technical discussions about pot rims and projectile points. There are popular journalism articles which breathe life into the subject, but these all suffer from brevity and a less-than-comprehensive look at data supporting the general gloss of their presentation. Few are the scholars outside the disciplines of archaeology and anthropology who have looked at the pre-contact Amerindian material. Joseph Campbell and Mircea Eliade did, of course; but then, what did they not look at in their many years of wide-ranging thinking about the origins of myth, symbol, icon, and religion.

Not until 1982 was it possible to find an inter-disciplinary discussion of pre-contact Amerindian material — the selected readings compiled in the anthology *Native North American Art History*, edited by Zena Pearlstone Mathews and Aldona Jonaitis. It is appropriate that this volume, bringing together writings from art historians, archaeologists, and anthropologists, be classified under the heading "art history." Art history, like the history of religion, is a syncretic, synthesizing field of inquiry. The work of a religious historian, however, was included in the anthology.

In 1985, two of the 28 authors collected in the Mathews and Jonaitis text (James A. Brown, anthropologist, and David W. Penney, art historian) combined forces with a third scholar (David S. Brose, archaeologist) to produce the year-long travelling exhibition: "Ancient Art of the American Woodland Indians." The exhibition opened March 17, 1985 at the National

Gallery of Art in Washington, then went on to the Detroit Institute of Arts, before closing March 12, 1986 at the Houston Museum of Fine Arts.

"Ancient Art of the American Woodland Indians" was an unprecedented event. The exhibition brought together for the first time grave goods scattered about in regional museums, state inventories, local historical societies, private collections, and university curio cabinets from Massachusetts to Oklahoma. The accompanying catalogue for the exhibition was worked to best scholarly standards, lavishly produced with high-quality colour plates and black-and-white reproductions, *and* wonderfully readable. The exhibition was not, however, a "blockbuster exhibition," not on the order of the Picasso and Tutankhamen exhibitions of the late 1970s. It failed to capture the general public's imagination.

There was a time, however, when anything at all to do with the mound builders did exert strong pull on popular imagination. During the nineteenth century, Sunday afternoon excavators abounded in the meadows and fields of much of the United States (see fig. 6). There was a whole genre of popular romance stories based on mound builder speculation. The public's titillating interest in mounds and mound builders enhanced the early credibility of the founders of the Church of the Latter Day Saints, the Mormons who believe the angel Moroni's golden tablets were buried in a mound, the hill called "Cumorah." Everybody had a theory about the mound builders, who they were — Vikings, the lost tribe of Israel, wandering Irish, Hernando de Soto and his men, even perhaps prehistoric Masons, if one can imagine it — but not Indians. That was not possible to imagine. The surviving Indians known to the European colonizers and their descendants could not have been the long-lost, ancient mound builders. Nevertheless, conscientious scholarship plodded on throughout the nineteenth century, and by the turn of this century, scholars had pretty much concluded that the almost unthinkable was true. The mound builders were Indians, perhaps the ancestors of the "five civilized tribes," the local Indians removed not that long ago to the Indian Territory — the Creek, Cherokee, Choctaw, Seminole, and Chickashaw. Interest in knowing more about the mound builders died fast. The glory of the treasure dulled.

I believe that the political context and economic pressures of the times had something to do with the fast fade of public interest. In the 1820s, unabated pressure for Indian lands in the southeastern United States resulted in Andrew Jackson's Indian Removal Act of 1830, a change in federal Indian policy that culminated in the forcible removal by the end of the decade of the Cherokee, Chickashaw, Choctaw, Creek, and Seminole Indians to the Indian Territory west of the Mississippi, a diaspora of over 100,000, known today as the "trail of tears." More than a fourth died as they were marched westward, many in manacles, under armed guard. In the 1890s the tribal governments were dissolved, the Indian Territory renamed Oklahoma, and the federal lands reallocated to non-Indian settlers in the great land rush of 1899. In 1907 Oklahoma, the "Sooner State," was admitted to statehood. No Indian benefited by these legal machinations. Geronimo, the great leader of the Chiricahua Apache of Arizona, died at Fort Sill, Oklahoma in 1908, his family exiled to Alabama, himself an excommunicate of the Dutch Reformed Church, the federal government having foresworn its earlier promise to relocate the Apache to Florida. But then, all Indians looked alike once upon a time not very long ago.

Not until the 1970s did trained researchers in any number begin to look again at the ancient earthworks of the mound builders. At least two factors spurred renewed interest.

First, federal dollars for capital construction projects, such as sewage lines or highway systems, required that environmental assessment studies be undertaken before any construction started. This legislation prompted routine "salvage archaeological" surveys with oftentimes surprising results. People just did not know what they had been sitting on top of all along. As a result, local and state historical societies, museums, universities, and community groups became powerful advocates of preservation. Secondly, the Amerindian peoples found themselves once again the objects of a romantic renewal of American interest in the "forest primeval" and "the noble savage." This interest was partly a spin-off of the Black civil rights movement, which had expanded to include such other disadvantaged groups as women, Hispanics, the disabled, and the elderly (so why not Indians), partly an outcome of a middle-class, white, youth drug culture (Indians know about peyote, mescal, etc.), and partly a general awareness of ecological problems (again, the "forest primeval"). Nonetheless, if the truth be told, the Indian burial mounds today are of limited interest even to the somewhat informed. They are scraggly, wooded, overgrown for the most part. They are not very glamorous. If one knows nothing about them—and few do—these poor, dull hillocks are easily ignored when seen at ground level. Survey drawings, however beautifully drafted, distort. They are bird's eye views. We do not see the work as it was meant to be seen. Much, so much, has been destroyed. One is far more likely to graduate from university today in North America knowing something about Egypt and Mesopotamia than about Cahokia and its population of 75,000, *the* North American trading, cultural, and religious center for hundreds of years. That is because we have learned imaginative responses to Old World archaic cultures. We grow up with tales of the pyramids and their mummies. Sadly, however, we lack almost any comprehension at all about what it might-have-been-like-way-back-then for the traditional New World cultures of this very land we ourselves now inhabit.

At one time it was estimated there were as many as 10,000 mounds just in the Ohio Valley alone.[18] Many are no longer visible at ground level because they have been plowed back; however, aerial surveys spot them rather easily. The soil is different where a mound was piled high; when the building material is earth, purposeful intention remains to be seen, even thousands of years later. Sacred spaces have a way of persisting, despite neglect.

The Sunwise Direction

To make an equivalence then between east and the rising sun and to call that equivalence "sacred" means, I believe, several things: It is an expression of hope that the sun will rise and warm the earth; it is a commemoration that the sun rose yesterday; and it is a thanksgiving that the sun has risen today. There is nothing observably certain about the sun rising at all. Eclipses do occur. Myths, in fact, tell of times the sun did not rise. Moreover, depending upon the time of year and the place of observation, the sun may seem to rise variously anywhere in the eastern quadrant of the sky, from northeast to southeast. In fact, if one is far enough north, the sun rises in the south. The night sky, too, appears to be guided by the movement of the sun—east to south to west to north. All things in the night sky move easterly, "sunwise"—east to south to west to north—the evening star rising in the west and travelling to the east by morning. To the night watcher, even the moon appears to travel east throughout the night.[19] It, too, disappears regularly and sometimes even irregularly.

All of these observations were everyday ones to people who watched for them ordinarily. One suspects after a study of the Amerindian extant material that at no time of the day or night was the ancient Amerindian unaware of a celestial calendar, of the sun's movement across the sky. Further, it mattered. So, too, should the dead in their sun-warmed burial mounds remain aware, renewed, recreated. In this respect, the ancient mound builders are part of a religious continuum observed worldwide among traditional peoples—a connectedness with earth and sun.

In the following pages I argue that the ancient Amerindian mound-building peoples created sacred landscapes by orienting their burial sites to the east, the direction of the rising sun, because central to their beliefs was a connectedness between the rising sun, an earth interment, and a renewal of life itself, perhaps even a transmigration. This directionality was an essential dimension of their highly religious *Weltanschauungen*; further, a sacred equivalence between east and the rising sun persists today.

Endnotes Chapter I

1. "Survey of Alberta may answer Questions about New World," *The Ottawa Citizen*, January 1, 1987, p. F-18. The Archaeological Survey of Alberta began a five-year project in 1987 to determine when and how many waves of migration there may have been, and just as importantly whether or not there was an ice-free corridor along the eastern slopes of the Rockies to enable early wanderers to move readily onto the plains and eastward along the great rivers to the woodlands of the east. Alberta has approximately 18,000 confirmed archaeological sites.

2. Jaime de Angulo, *Coyote Man and Old Doctor Loon* (San Francisco: Turtle Island Foundation, 1973). Jaime de Angulo worked for many years as an anthropologist among the Pit River Indians of northern California. They had little material culture of note and lived in such lodges in one of the most barren, remote parts of California. De Angulo considered the Pit River Indians to be Stone Age survivors.

3. Robert Silverberg, *Mound Builders of Ancient America* (Greenwich: New York Graphics Society, 1968), p. 231; William T. Sanders and Joseph Marino, *New World Prehistory* (Englewood Cliffs: Prentice-Hall, 1970), p. 27: "Charcoal samples from supposed hearths in North American sites have been found by C14 method to date from between 38,000 and 22,000 years ago. None of these claims has been fully accepted by American archaeologists."

4. Joseph Campbell, *The Masks of Gods: Primitive Mythology* (New York: Penguin Books, 1969), p. 395.

5. John A. Eddy, "Medicine Wheels and Plains Indian Astronomy," in *Native American Astronomy*, edited by Anthony Aveni (Austin: University of Texas Press, 1975), p. 148.

6. *Ibid.*, p. 149.

7. Thomas Kehoe and Alice B. Kehoe, "Stones, Solstices, and Sun Dance Structures," *Plains Anthropologist* 22 (1976), p. 87.

8. Eddy, *op.cit.*, p. 149.

9. Kehoe and Kehoe, *op.cit.*, p. 91.

10. Eddy, *op.cit.*, p. 152.

11. Kehoe and Kehoe, *op.cit.*, pp. 86-87.

12. Eddy, *op.cit.*, p. 159.

13. *Ibid.*, p. 161.

14. Thaddeus M. Cowan, "Effigy Mounds and Stellar Representation: A comparison of Old World and New World alignment schemes," in *Archaeoastronomy in Pre-Columbian America*, edited by Anthony F. Aveni (Austin: University of Texas Press, 1977), pp. 217-234.

15. Travis Hudson and Ernest Underhay, *Crystals in the Sky: An intellectual odyssey involving Chumash astronomy, cosmology, and rock art* (Ballena: Anthropological Papers X, 1978).

16. P. Clay Sherrod and Martha Ann Rolingson, *Surveyors of the Ancient Mississippi Valley* (Little Rock, Arkansas: Arkansas Archeological Survey Research Series, no. 28, 1987.

17. Robert Silverberg's *Mound Builders of Ancient America* (1968) is a comprehensive history of the research, from the first accounts of the European explorers to the nineteenth-century theories proposed, debunked, and the twentieth-century ebb and flow of scholarly and popular interest as people have sought to preserve what remains for reasons they still know not why.

18. Robert Claibourne, *The Emergence of Man: The first Americans* (New York: Time-Life Books, 1973), p. 127.

19. The supposed "eastern" route of the moon at night is an optical illusion.

Chapter II

THE MOUND BUILDERS

This chapter sketches ancient mound-building activity in the Mississippi Valley. It describes what the mounds looked like and what has been found inside them for a period of time from c.1,500 BCE, Poverty Point, to Cahokia, c.1,200 CE, the grandest of the Mississippian sites. The reader's ...attention is directed to persistent similarities in the physical appearance of the earthworks and the objects found inside them, as well as to the characteristics differentiating the several mound-building cultures — Poverty Point, Adena, Hopewell, and Mississippian. Although researchers have over the years found much to argue about concerning the mound-building peoples, from the broadest possible point of view all of these North American cultures participated in a religious continuum found worldwide: they built mounds, created sacred landscapes.

Mound-building Techniques

Mound-building techniques worldwide are not dissimilar. Some sacred object is always enclosed. A pit is dug, lined, a sacred object placed within, a superstructure formed about it; then earth or clay piled over. The process may be repeated to build the mound higher. The oldest mounds appear to be conical in form with a carefully smoothed surface. Mounds of a later date may take different forms — effigy figures, geometrical shapes — or be combinations of shapes; however, the conical or loaf form is never entirely supplanted by these later innovations.

The earliest-known example of mound building anywhere, as might be expected, is not found in the New World. Square 10Q is a composite construction located only a few years ago, on the northwest coast of Spain.

There is a small, single-chamber cave near Santander called El Juyo.[1] Within the cave is a composite construction, Square 10Q. It is a mound. Only a meter high, the mound consists of alternating layers of charred sacrificial bones and columns of coloured clays, arranged in seven-part rosettes. White, red, yellow, and green clays were used, the whole of the mound coated with yellow clay and covering four square meters. A trench dug around the mound was filled with limpet and periwinkle shells.

What is interesting about this construction is that similar sorts of mound-building techniques were used ever so much later in the New World—coloured clays, the layering of artifacts, burnt bones, seashells, circle arrangements, trenches and columns. What these particular techniques meant formally in the Magdalenian period, no one really knows, of course. Nevertheless, they do mean, however, that there was "a right way" of doing things. The raising of a mound (even when inside a cave) honours the objects inside the mound in a different way than interring those objects in the earth, or leaving them in a tree, or consigning them to a river, or simply placing them on the ground. It is obvious that for long periods of time in very different areas, people have apparently been making similar decisions about how to build a mound and what goes inside a mound. One can only assume that the problems prompting those decisions were also similar because the solutions seem specific, particular, not random.

Poverty Point

What little land there was in the Mississippi delta which remained dry underfoot throughout the year was intensively used. The earliest example we have of mound-building activity and of a settled population sustained partly by agriculture (sunflower and other plants),[2] plus hunting and fishing, comes from this region—Poverty Point, Louisiana. It is a startling example to our modern eye. William Sears calls Poverty Point "...a specialization that stands alone in the Southeast."[3] But it does not stand completely alone.

Poverty Point lies on a tall bluff overlooking the Bayou Maçon to the east, and the Arkansas River 7 m below (figs. 7, 8). It is a sequence of five to six concentric arcs extending 1,300 m across at the outside and 650 m across on the inside.[4] The arcs define a plaza that fronts onto the bluff. For many years it has been assumed that the construction visible today is only half of what there was originally—either six concentric rings or octagons—because the site was thought to have been severely eroded by the

Arkansas River. Very recently, the Louisiana Archaeological Survey and Antiquities Commission concluded the site is intact, the "...bluff that marks the eastern edge of the site today and which seems to have been cut into the earthwork was formed thousands of years before building ever started."[5] The arcs are truncated ridges about 2 m tall and 17 m to 50 m wide. Upon the ridges stood houses, individual dwellings probably. There are four causeways or avenues that cut through the arcs to the plaza. They do not divide the arcs into four equal wedges, nor do the avenues converge at one point anywhere, even theoretically. The avenues are 12 m to 50 m wide.

Some authorities speculate the avenues were used in astronomical alignments not unlike Stonehenge. Two of the avenues appear to align with summer and winter solstices.[6] Moreover, there are postholes in the plaza which may indicate other astronomical markers such as equinoxes.[7] If so, then we have here a major earthworks calendar that is not only roughly contemporaneous with Stonehenge but exhibits certain similar design solutions. For example, the Stonehenge avenue, built c.2,100 BCE and extended to the river c.1,100 BCE, was widened to align it with the summer solstice sunrise.[8]

A very large, irregular mound 22.5 m high is connected by a 7 m high platform to the outer arc on the west. The mound has been described as a bird effigy,[9] "...oriented westward with wings extended, thereby paralleling the daily route of the sun."[10] If so, it is a unique depiction. The Louisiana Archaeological Survey, in fact, refers to it as a "monster structure"[11] and thinks the bird identification suspect. I tend to agree. There are no other bird effigy mounds built anywhere later that even approach this design.[12]

The height of the Poverty Point mound may be more important for our present discussion than its shape. From its summit, it has an unobstructed view over the ridges, the broad plaza, out over the bayou, out to the east, and to the rising sun. By 1,000 BCE, as many as 2,000 or more people lived at Poverty Point. The site was occupied for over 1,000 years. It took several generations to build. One researcher has estimated that 30 million loads of dirt, each 25 kg, were carried from nearby "borrow pits" to construct the mounds and ridges.[13]

As dramatic as the site appears to our eyes today, it was only the grandest of many Poverty Point culture sites along the Mississippi River and its tributaries, all with at least one dome-shaped mound built in layers, sometimes as many as eight, all with a cleared plaza fronting the mound(s), sometimes with embankments which connected mounds, served as house foundations, or were astronomical alignments of some   sort (still to be worked out).[14] Poverty Point is no longer thought to be a "...geographical or developmental irregularity."[15] It is part of the Archaic period which extended from about 3,000 BCE well into historic times in some parts of North America. It was the architectural beginning in North America of something we recognize to be religious — formal burial rites.

Poverty Point cultural influence encompasses an area from Florida to Louisiana and north to Tennessee and Missouri, all of it interconnected via river systems.[16] Somewhere around 3,000 BCE trading or migratory routes had been formed extending throughout North America along all of the great rivers, from the Gulf Coast to the Great Lakes, from Florida to the Maritimes, and westward to the Rockies. These trading and migratory routes made Poverty Point the important center it was for so many years.

Other Archaic Period Burial Sites

There were other important Archaic sites, also. From the northeast alone, so many artifacts have been found that Robert Funk writes: "It is almost as if an 'explosion' had occurred in population and/or intensity (stability) of occupation...."[17] James Fitting also comments on the "...spectacular increase in both the quantity and the complexity of archaeological materials,"[18] and James Tuck calls it an "...outburst of mortuary ceremonialism."[19]

Typically, the Archaic period burial is formal, ritualistic, often a flexed inhumation, sometimes a cremation.[20] Red ochre (sometimes yellow) is used for anointing, and the burial site is an east-facing,[21] elevated[22] site. Grave goods are numerous and important, objects rare and valuable. There are gorgets and beads made of shell and copper in profusion, finely made stone tools, bannerstones, rattles and flutes, quartz pebbles, and amulets. James Tuck believes the amulets are part of the rituals used in hunting magic because they are variously "...the feet and bills of diving birds, the claws and teeth of seals, bear, caribou, fox, or beaver, and less easily interpreted objects of crystal, stone, and bone."[23] Hunting magic or possibly curing magic, too, must be considered because these same items are historically ones associated with shamanism. Whatever the specific meaning intended, the grave goods so interred must have been thought useful for the afterlife or the journey ahead.[24]

Bodies were prepared for interment by anointing them with red ochre. If cremated, the charred remains of the corpse were collected and anointed with red ochre, then interred with grave goods.[25] Red ochre has been used in this manner in many cultures back to the age of proto Cro-magnon and the Neanderthal, 100,000 to 40,000 years ago. Ochre is a strong preservative. One must imagine that it was important then that the skin and bone not decay immediately. Were there rites that could only be said at certain times of the year to ensure safe journey? Was it a journey of many days that the dead would undertake? The use of red ochre — red, the life-giving, ritual colour — almost always tells us even more emphatically than the grave goods that belief in another life was a strongly held belief for which protective measures were undertaken on behalf of the dead. The impulse or requirement to care for the dead is a religious ethic almost by definition.

Throughout all of the northeast, the Maritimes, the Great Lakes region, and down into the Mississippi valley, similar Archaic period burial practices can be identified and dated to sometime between 3,000 BCE and 1,500 BCE.[26] James Tuck argues that these burial practices probably have a northern origin since no evidence of a like burial cult has been found in the southeastern United States,[27] the Poverty Point areas. Only a few instances of interment in mounds, all cremations, have been located to date. These would have been status burials of some sort. There is another possibility, however, to explain the absence of more ordinary grave sites — their location.

Inland Archaic burial sites were usually near sizable, navigable (by dugout canoe)[28] waterways and, hence, remained attractive to later inhabitants in the same region. The Archaic burial site can be in or near a midden. Some of the midden heaps are as high as 1.5 m and extend over an acre.[29] These areas were returned to seasonally and habitually[30] for generations. One can imagine that the bones of honoured ancestors were part of the reason for return. Bones in the earth established a sacred territoriality, some part of the earth identified as one's own. The land was not barren. It brought forth new life seasonally. The ancestors were remembered in these places because their bones were the irreducible borderline between the human world and the spirit worlds above and below.[31]

Burial sites located in flood plains or on the seacoast have, of course, disappeared from knowledge for the most part, but not entirely. Several inhumations within oyster shell middens are known. One such site on Edisto Island, off the South Carolina coast, is dated to 1,900-1,200 BCE.[32] An important ceremonial purpose must be presumed. It consists of a single oyster shell ring[33] about 25 m in diameter and a crescent (or ring portion) opening northeast (see fig. 10). William N. Morgan reports that a similar ring has been found in Colombia on the Atlantic seacoast and has been dated to 3,000 BCE.[34] Other oyster shell configurations with burials along the Atlantic coast are known and dated to 2,240 BCE.[35]

From the grave goods and midden heaps we know fishing and foraging were supplements to hunting, not replacements; moreover, in particularly clement areas agriculture of some description was practiced. Grains and nuts were ground with mortars and pestles, dogs were domesticated,[36] pottery fired.

Adena and Hopewell Dispersal Routes

For most archaeologists, the development of pottery marks the end of the Archaic period. We can date that at about 2,000-1,000 BCE east of the Mississippi. Early Woodlands then would be about 1,000 BCE. Woodlands continues into historic times and is usually organized in terms of tribal affiliations — that is, subdivisions within the Woodlands and Plains tribal groups. There is an important exception, however. The people who left behind heroic effigies and mounds along the Mississippi and Ohio rivers and further north into Wisconsin are called "mound builders" because no one knows who the creators of the Adena, Hopewell, and Mississippian cultures[37] really were or where they went. Their earthwork constructions were not even initially noticed by the earliest explorers on the Mississippi River. They thought the region quite uninhabited.

During the Archaic period, people trod their accustomed routes in small bands;[38] somehow, around 1,500 BCE, and in some way we do not understand, some of these same people reorganized themselves into tribal configurations (as these terms are defined by Elman R. Service),[39] and others still later, refined the tribal configurations forming chiefdoms. One way or another, all three social groups produced elaborate funerary complexes over more than 2,500 years. Then they dispersed, along the great river routes, and in that diaspora carried part of their culture with them. Fragmented, shattered, or perhaps redefined, reformed.

The Adena traits were centered in southern Illinois and the Ohio Valley.[40] By 25 CE these traits could be found as far north as Lake Huron, as far east as Maryland, north into Michigan,[41] south to Alabama,[42] and along the St. Lawrence River.[43] According to James Tuck: "An actual migration of Adena people from the Ohio Valley to the Atlantic coast has been suggested by some archaeologists (Ritchie and Dragoo, 1959), while others

(Griffin, 1961) suggest diffusion or trade as the most reasonable explanation. Available carbon-14 dates favor the former theory, while increasing evidence of coastal-midwestern interaction throughout the Archaic period suggests that the latter theory may be correct."[44]

Hopewell traits followed a very similar route, leading many scholars to assume that one or more of the historic era Amerindian groups are the descendants of the Adena / Hopewell. A number of possibilities have been suggested, notably the Cherokee, Sioux, and the Algonkian groups.[45] The Algonkian and Cherokee are both known in historic times to have favoured an easterly orientation for their burial sites; the Sioux, like the Iroquois, favoured a westerly direction.

Overlap of Adena and Hopewell Time Periods

The Adena people are dated to about 1,000 BCE,[46] about 500 years after the decline of the Poverty Point culture, and continuing to 200 CE,[47] or about 1,200 years in sum. Alternately, some date Adena from 800 BCE to 800 CE.[48] Others think of Adena not so much as a separate culture, but as an enhancement of the Archaic period's burial cult practices,[49] centered locally in the Ohio Valley within a restricted core area having a radius of 240 km. Others in the same way see no clear division between Adena and Hopewell,[50] and some even posit a coexistence of Hopewell and Adena.[51] As Robert Silverberg writes: "From the C-14 evidence then, it appears now that these two mound-building cultures of the Ohio Valley flourished for about fifteen centuries, overlapping for most of the time, and both were in decay by the fifth century AD."[52]

The beginning of Hopewell culture is not so easily spotted as Adena. David Brose notes that anything to do with Ohio Hopewell (concentrated, that is, in the Scioto Valley) will be "...the least accurately dated,"[53] and could be anywhere in a broad range from 100 BCE to 600 CE. Mussel shell dates and bark dates confuse, and there is no clear pottery date demarcating Hopewell from Adena.[54] James Griffin accepts roughly 300 BCE as a start date for Illinois Hopewell, differentiating it from Ohio Hopewell at 100 BCE or later, and stressing the continuity of Adena and Hopewell. The range for a start date would appear then to be 300 BCE[55] to 1 CE,[56] with a decline noted beginning about 300 CE,[57] and 600 CE[58] or 800 CE[59] for a close, although one archaeologist carries the terminus forward to 1,000 CE.[60]

No suggestions are made as to what balance the relationship between coexistent Adena and Hopewell people might have been in an area such as the Scioto Valley; however, James Griffin suggests that the Hopewell were "...not politically or geographically aggressive."[61] It is usually felt that the reason for their dispersal and/or disappearance from the Ohio Valley is that both Adena and Hopewell were driven out by invading Iroquois. Hence, the last Hopewell structures built were palisaded hilltop forts.

Adena and Hopewell Burial Ritual

Adena burial mounds were often incorporated into Hopewell sites in the Scioto Valley of Ohio, and geometrical enclosures were almost an Ohio specialty.[62] Overlooking this Hopewell characteristic, Silverberg comments instead: "The chief difference between Adena and Hopewell burials lies not in the preparation of the tombs but in the greater richness and quality of the Hopewell accompanying grave goods."[63] He calls them "...the Egyptians of the United States,"[64] noting that found in one mound alone in Ohio were "...12,000 unperforated pearls, 35,000 pearl beads, 20,000 shell beads, and nuggets of copper, meteoric iron and silver as well as small sheets of hammered gold, copper, and iron beads, and more."[65]

Silverberg is perhaps overly impressed with the grave goods. More and better grave goods only means that there is a continuing desire to send along the very best with the dead so they shall not be found wanting in any way. It represents no difference in religious thought between Adena and Hopewell. Moreover, it is absolutely consistent with what we know of Archaic period burial procedures. If these grave goods seem more wonderful than ever it is only because the "Ohio Interaction Sphere," or trading routes, was even more successful in bringing rare and wonderful items into the Ohio Valley—such things as Great Lakes copper and Gulf Coast conch shells, grizzly bear teeth from the Rockies, chalcedony from the Dakotas, obsidian from the Yellowstone River area. None of these items are bulky, all could be carried by walkers following the routes of the great rivers. And they were. There is another much more important difference between Adena and Hopewell. The burial ritual itself changes. That means a change in expectation for the dead and what they may expect to encounter. What the change means we cannot be sure.

The change is this: Adena mounds were built up over generations of hereditary burial. Building an Adena mound was a long-term village project, as much for its size as for the number of bodies layered within. We can imagine that everyone in an Adena band expected to be returned to the earth, to the mound, and was—adult, child, male, female, all were interred, all returned.

The Hopewell mounds, just as large, appear to have been built in one go.[66] Ossuaries were added to the burial complex to collect bones until the proper time arrived to build a mound. Perhaps this means only that the Hopewell were more efficient about mound-building than the Adena. But for some archaeologists, the vastly increased number of cremations to whole body interments in a Hopewell mound (the ratio is 3:1) which this practice produced, suggests a "...form of retainer burial."[67] If so, we must consider the possibility that the later Mississippian practice of human sacrifice had its roots in Adena/Hopewell, not Mexico. Or, that we have here another argument for Mesoamerican influence earlier than what is usually presented if the "retainer burial" indicates a cult of sacrifice to propitiate the sun. There are paired interments of young men and women in the Hopewell mounds. Sacred space is similarly delineated in geometrical enclosures.

David Brose views the change from hereditary burial to élite burial as one demonstrating that the mound builders had chosen to emphasize status individuals "...who had been designated by the familial/political group to mediate between society and cosmic/spiritual beings."[68] For Brose this sort of élite selection also means "...a coincident change from the mobile, diffuse hunting/fishing/gathering economies of the Middle Woodlands to the relatively permanent agricultural societies that presaged the Mississippian period."[69] It is not that certain, however, that Hopewell was so agriculturally based.

Interestingly enough, though, in Illinois towards the end of the Hopewell period, when mound-building activity generally declines, the élite mound burial is replaced by small familial burials in stone heaps.[70] One researcher identifies at this time an increased "ritual energy" in male burials in at least one area in Illinois,[71] suggesting a differentiation in the earlier elaboration of the mound burial might be traced to sex as a later development. More work needs to be done, however, in this area before any status separation can be stated derived from sexual differences.

Unlike Adena settlements which are easily associated with their burial mounds because the settlement is nearby the mound, the Hopewell villages were at such a remove from the sacred province that for a long time archaeologists did not know if the Hopewell mound builders lived in villages. Some researchers thought them possibly as nomadic as the paleo-Indian.[72] Finally, permanent Hopewell settlements were located. They, like the Adena sites, showed a long period of occupation and, importantly, many non-mound burials.[73] In other words, not all Hopewell were interred in mounds. One suspects from later Woodlands practice that the first to be excluded from the communion of mound builders were children. They had not built the mounds. Perhaps that was why. Perhaps they did not have to earn their way back home to the earth. There is no way to know.

Mesoamerican Influence in Adena / Hopewell

Lastly, there are those who discern a Mesoamerican influence in Hopewell not present in Adena. The argument is inconclusive and rests on finding similarities in central Mexican ballfields and Hopewell-enclosed earthworks and in the possibility of a ritual human sacrifice to the sun in Hopewell ceremonies as there was in Mesoamerica. To date, the best evidence seems to be a like unit of measurement found in both Hopewell structures and in Teotihuacan—62 m as a unit;[74] however, it is not the intention of my study to review and assess the argument for Mesoamerican influence in Adena / Hopewell.

A Physical Description of the Burial Mound

The Adena burial mound is tall, steep-sided, and conical; so, too, the Hopewell mound. Some Hopewell mounds have flattened tops. The Adena mound stands alone on a cleared plain on a high bluff overlooking a river, which is usually to the east. The Hopewell mound is often one of many gathered within a sacred enclave also on a high bluff overlooking a river to the east.

Irregular cryptic earthworks, meandering ridges of earth actually, are often associated with the Adena burial mound (see fig. 11). These forms are reminiscent of glyphs etched in rock on the Peterborough site in Ontario, a site dated variously as early as 3,500 years ago[75] and as recently as 900-1,400 CE.[76] Sometimes the Adena ridges are simple circular enclosures about the base of the mound, or concentric circles, not very tall, and absolutely round.

Hopewell earthworks, too, are often round, a perfect circle, but always much larger than Adena. The largest Adena circle was measured to about

168 m. A Hopewell circular enclosure typically measures 400 m for its diameter. Hopewell earth ridge designs tend to stress a symmetry of form for each unit — e.g., parallel lines, not meanders; squared, compressed octagonal figures, not kinked, circular spirals — although the joining of each Hopewell design unit on a cleared field results often in a complex asymmetry (see fig. 12).

An Adena burial mound can be as tall as the 22 m mound at Miamisburg, Ohio (see fig. 13), but usually an Adena mound is smaller, about 7 m to 10 m. The Hopewell burial mound can be just as tall. There seems, too, to have been a serious effort to use the earth itself as a decorative feature on the mound's exterior finish. The surface is often a patchwork of yellow, red, brown colour created by the clayey earth hauled basket by basket to the site from borrow pits which can be located even today.[77] According to Ann Daniel-Hartung, referring to the later building of the Cahokia mounds, "Most of the mound building was done by women carrying earth-laden baskets weighing 35 to 50 pounds."[78] Daniel-Hartung's contention may find support in historic Cherokee practice: women are known to have been the ones to build small burial mounds by carrying earth in baskets.[79]

Interment, including Cremation

Within the mounds were burials. Small mounds might contain only one grave, usually an important interment, the corpse laid in an extended position, often laid out so the face of the centered corpse would greet the rising sun, the body covered with red ochre. Others are more complex. A typical Adena mound started as a pit burial in a log-faced tomb with one or more corpses arranged by status about the centered ones. The pit was enclosed and covered with earth. By the addition of more bodies or another log tomb platform, and more earth covering, the mound could be raised higher and higher until a tall, steep, conical slope was obtained. Some corpses were cremated and may be less important figures because they are found at the same level as other inhumations in the mound.[80] The ashes were interred in clay-lined basins which had been used for the cremation.[81] On the other hand, they might simply have been people who had died earlier and whose bones had been preserved for interring in the mound when the next one was built, or the one in current use opened and readied for receipt of more interments.

Cremations followed the stripping of rotted flesh from the bones.[82] In historic times, the Choctaw Indians had religious functionaries — sometimes men, sometimes women—who were the tribe's honoured flesh strippers, travelling from village to village to perform this ritual deed properly as part of the Choctaw feast of the dead.[83] The flesh was distributed among the Choctaw fields, a good source of soil nutrients, and another allusion to the return of flesh to the earth to ensure fertility and new growth. The bones were preserved in an ossuary or charnel house, which in time was heaped over with earth to form a burial mound. In 1636 Father LeJeune described the Lake Simcoe Huron feast of the dead.[84] It was similar. He noted that the feast was held every 12 years or so since that was as long as the tribe was likely to stay in any one part of the forest. They would bring all the bones together of all who had died in the tribe since the last feast of the dead and place the bones in a common pit with much ritual and devotion. Those who were only recently dead had the flesh carved from their bones.

As before, all interments, including those consisting of cremated remains, were anointed with red ochre,[85] and sometimes graphite.[86]

Multiple burials on one level might have one corpse extended and centered and other corpses, extended or flexed, laid in a surround on the four sides of the centered corpse. The Adena people were tall, women 2 m or more, men as tall as 2.5 m[87] and round-headed. Round-headedness has led some to speculate that Adena people were new stock in the valley, different from other Archaic peoples and from Hopewell who were long-headed. It could be, however, only that one group wrapped their babies differently on a cradleboard, resulting in a more "round-headed" appearance. Further, the sample of "round-headedness" is small, based on less than a hundred skulls. If the Adena ruling families were once especially tall, they could stay that way through careful marriage. The Ohio Hopewell skulls certainly suggest that only one family was important in this area: the richest burial deposits all contain skulls having the same genetically transmitted bony growth, an *epostoses*.[88]

Some graves are flexed burials covered by stone tablets, and some were buried in a seated position alone facing east or in groups in semi-circles or circles. One Adena burial of twelve people[89] was discovered in a mound on a bluff overlooking the Mississippi in Jo Davies county, Illinois. All twelve figures were seated in a circle in a stone vaulted crypt, their backs to the walls, and in the center a large conch shell beaker. The crypt was divided into three sections. The twelve were in the middle. On either side were sealed cells, filled with a brown dust of reportedly horrid stench. Although there has never been an identification, one assumes it consisted of blood and other fleshy remains (see fig. 14). This particular exhumation gave rise to certain nineteenth-century declarations that here, indeed, was the answer to who were the mound builders because these figures had been buried in the ancient way of the Masonic rite. The mound builders, therefore, were prehistoric Masons.

Grave Goods

Long-distance trade continued to support the funerary practice of interring rare and important items with the deceased. Wonderful items have been found in Adena mounds and in Hopewell mounds. Unfortunately, most of the grave goods were excavated in the nineteenth century by enthusiastic treasure-hunters so we have unreliable records, if any, of how these items and the corpses and other remains were arranged within the mounds.

Grave goods include Gulf Coast conch shell beakers, jewelry made of Lake Superior copper and meteorite iron.[90] There are beautiful bannerstones and birdstones, mica cutouts, highly polished, incised sandstone and limestone tablets (see Appendix A), zoomorphic platform and tubular pipes, pottery urns and figures. Late in the Hopewell period elbow pipes appear.[91] Several antler headdresses have been found. For the most part, they consist of deer or elk antlers; but, according to Robert Silverberg, some were cut from hammered copper.[92] The antler headdress worldwide is an important part of the shaman's gear. In the Huron creation myth, Good Brother is only able to kill Evil Brother (however temporarily) with a deer's antler, thus restoring order to the world.[93] And as long ago as Trois Frères, a similarly masked deer-man, commemorated in a wall painting, also displayed this totemic intimacy with the spirits.

Settled Adena / Hopewell Communities

Somewhat at a remove from the Adena burial mound complex was the Adena village. Its houses, like the burial mounds, were "...perfectly round, being built of posts that were set into the ground in spaced pairs and slanted outward from the base," according to R. F. Spencer and James Jennings.[94] The houses were made of willow, roofed with slabs of bark,[95] or thatch,[96] 7 m to 28 m in diameter.[97] Hopewell houses appear to have been built similarly,[98] although late in the period they became rectangular.[99] The Adena people harvested grain, but it is not certain if they planted, and if so, what. Likely cultigens, however, would have been squash, gourds, and sunflowers, possibly pumpkin,[100] even corn.[101] Adena settlements were not migratory hunting camps.[102] Nor were Hopewell settlements. In fact, Hopewell probably were corn growers,[103] although that is by no means certain, either.[104] Hunting and fishing were the predominant food sources supplementing everyday foraging. The smaller Adena settlements suggest that people were organized into bands. The Scioto Valley Hopewell people were probably a tribe[105] by this time. It is possible that was true for the Adena of the same time also.

In summary, what we have here then is an association of agriculture with settled communities, very likely a tribal structure, but two somewhat different sets of burial practice coexistent in the same area. One group buried everybody as they died incrementally in the same mound, adding to the mound as needed; another group held off erecting a burial mound until there was someone important or wealthy enough to warrant one, then buried everyone together, some more importantly accompanied by grave goods than others. Both Adena and Hopewell raised conical mounds on cleared plains with associated earthwork on similar sites. In fact, Hopewell often incorporated Adena structures into their sites, or maybe it was *vice versa*.

The Mississippian Temple Shrine

On the heels of Adena / Hopewell came the Mississippian culture (also called Temple Mound), dated from 600 CE,[106] 700 CE,[107] or 900 CE,[108] and ranging from 1,000 CE (for the St. Louis to Vicksburg stretch of the Mississippi River)[109] to 1,400 CE.[110]

It was a true chiefdom with sumptuary rules, social stratification, and a priesthood. The Mississippian culture was organized in this fashion by 1,000 CE,[111] if not before. All community activity was centered on the temple shrine, which was an ancestor shrine, and the residence of the ruler known by "...his descent from the solar diety via a line of past rulers."[112] The ossuary *cum* treasury containing the bones of the ruler's ancestors and their grave offerings was an important part of the shrine.[113] Because several Mississippian centers survived into historic times—the Calusa of Florida, the Cofitachequi of Georgia, the Natchez of Mississippi, and the

Powhatan of Virginia[114] — there are first-hand reports from early European explorers describing Mississippian customs.

Mississippian is different from Adena/Hopewell in a number of ways. It came from the south[115] into the great river valley up the Mississippi, following the old Adena-Hopewell interaction route, and eventually spreading out to encompass all of the old territory and more under its influence which lasted throughout the southeast until contact with the marauding Spanish explorers. The Mississippians built mounds — mounds of an astounding size, temple mounds and platform mounds, not just burial mounds. The burial mounds were relatively minor features of the mortuary complex. They added truncated pyramids to the earthwork vocabulary — in other words, terraced earth platforms arranged about plazas. Upon these platforms they built temples, élite residences (completely unlike the Adena/Hopewell practice), storage buildings, and in so doing, they rearranged tribal concepts about the use of public space. For example, at the Angel site (Evansville, Indiana) on the north bank of the Ohio River, an estimated 1,000 people lived in 200 houses[116] whose corners were all oriented to compass points,[117] albeit not to cardinal points. Doors opened on the east-facing walls; the most important mound, a three-level terraced structure, was oriented to the northeast. Its directional orientation is echoed in the 300 burials found to date, all of which are extended or flexed burials and exhibit a northeast to southeast alignment.[118] It is important to note also that in this site the northeast directional preference is a more important directional factor than the Ohio River (see fig. 15).

The Mississippian architecture was courtly, priestly, ceremonial, urban, and urbane, and relatively short-lived compared to Adena / Hopewell.

Cahokia

Cahokia is thought to have been the premier Mississippian center. Its development overlapped with Adena / Hopewell, no matter how that period is dated. Some Adena / Hopewell carry-overs can be identified, in addition to the presumed Mesoamerican influence — although it must be noted that Nelson Reed thinks an "...excellent argument can be made for an indigenous development of these two traits [flat-top mounds arranged around a plaza] together with superficial convergence."[119] His is, however, a minority viewpoint. The Cahokia settlement at its peak, c.1,000 CE to 1,250 CE, had a population of perhaps 38,000 and possibly as many as 75,000 if the surrounding area is included in the estimate.[120] Some Mississippian ceremonial centers were ringed by farming villages.   People may have moved back and forth between village and ceremonial center throughout the year. Village houses were eclectic in construction—round, oval, or rectangular.[121]   They were built of wattle-and-daub.[122]   Both villages and ceremonial centers were usually protected by palisades.[123]

At Cahokia, there were an estimated 120 mounds[124] in an area of about 1500 ha. The largest mound is "Monks Mound." Its height is 34 m, 10 stories tall, and covers an area of about 5.6 ha. Monks Mound, according to C-14 dates, is estimated to have been built between 900 CE and 1,200 CE.[125] It may have been built by women, only by women, who carried baskets of earth, each weighing 17 kg to 25 kg. Monks Mound has a mass larger than the Pyramid of Khufu in Egypt. Soil samples indicate that it was built in 14 stages, the oldest layer starting at 7 m and reaching 34 m in four terraces about 1,150 CE.[126] Some of the mounds were conical burial sites, just as they had been for Adena / Hopewell, with accompanying charnel houses on platform mounds,[127] connected to the burial mound by a ridge of earth—much as may have been the case at Poverty Point so long before. The grandeur of Monks Mound is heightened, too, when one realizes that not only was it tallest of the Cahokia groups, but half of the estimated 120 mounds were *under* 3.5 m.[128]

Mississippians grew corn, of this there is no doubt.[129] They had a flint hoe, an important agricultural tool.[130]   The corn originally came from Mexico, and by 900 CE it was a dietary staple.[131]

Where Adena / Hopewell had relied upon the spear and spearthrower, or atlatl,[132] Mississippians used the more efficient bow and arrow. It was introduced into the Ohio Valley area by 700 CE.[133] They may have been a more combative people than the Adena / Hopewell,[134] or they were under more pressure from the north than we know.

Some archaeologists view Cahokia as a pottery manufacturing center. Theirs was a distinctive, high-quality pottery, often in the form of human or animal effigies. Others cite the importance of the Mississippian flint hoe and see Cahokia as a manufacturing center for that implement. No doubt there are several items which formed the basis of the trade exchange that filled the Mississippian tombs with valuable items from far-flung areas.[135]

"Southern Death Cult" Motifs

The development of what is called variously the "Southeastern Ceremonial Complex,"[136] the "Southern Death Cult,"[137] and the "Southern Cult"[138] may have encompassed an area from Georgia to Oklahoma. It is not well understood at all. As defined by James A. Brown, a cult is "...a formalized set of rites dedicated to the veneration or propitiation of specific individuals, spirits, or forces."[139] That is an archaeologist's definition, not one used by a historian of religion who would describe such activities as simply "religious." There was a priesthood (male and/or female, we do not know), whose elaborate ceremonials, centered on the temple shrine, seem little connected to the religious rite of Adena/Hopewell.[140] The shrines held images of one or more male figures, some had images of male and female figures.[141] We need not assume that these were the Mississippian "gods." Perhaps they were images of gods. Perhaps they were only placed there to commemorate and protect the bones of the ancestors[142] — and not "godly" at all. How are we to know? We do not. What we do know, as Mircea Eliade reminds us, is that "...on the archaic levels of culture, the real — that is, the powerful, the meaningful, the living — is equivalent to the sacred."[143] The "real" then is those "sacred bones." Be they Adena, Hopewell, or Mississippian, they belong to someone who has died. But red ochre preserves; fire transcends; earth revivifies because the bones are placed in the earth. There is no inherent contradiction in burning or not burning the bones first even if cremation is usually thought of as a means of sending the spirit aloft because these bones, or ashes, are consistently returned to the earth. We must, therefore, understand the mound itself to be an animating agent, a multivalent agent. In Eliade's words: "An essential characteristic of religious symbolism is its multivalence, its capacity to express simultaneously a number of meanings."[144]

There are other examples. Åke Hultkrantz has traced Ohio Valley influence, particularly Mississippian, westward along the Missouri River to later ritual of the Pawnee, Arikara, Hidatsa, and Mandan tribes,[145] and to the Sioux, Omaha, Oto, Missouri, and Ponca:[146] for example, the altar square, the pipe, medicine bundle use, the human sacrifice of a maiden as evening star to the morning star,[147] and much of the sun-directional symbolism of the sun dance. Without question its elements are sun-directional, requiring one to honour the sun in order to be recreated, made new, and the pre-eminent direction in the ritual is east. The iconography of the sun dance is complex, layered, no one exegesis authoritative. Nonetheless, in Hultkrantz's understanding of Shoshoni ritual expecially, the sun dance pole is the cosmic pole, world tree, "backbone of the world," Milky Way, and "main path of communication between the god and the human creature."[148] This was possible because the ceremonial camp circle or *huthuga*, was "...conceived as a house, had an opening in the east, and contained the Sky people in its northern half and the Earth people in its southern half."[149] Sky people were responsible for the spiritual welfare of the nation and Earth people for their physical welfare[150] — two halves of an integrated whole if there were to be peace.

James Brown also describes several historic period religious practices of the Plains tribes, particularly the use of shell masks and war bundles, as "...condensed symbols of sacred ancestral power"[151] which have survived from the Mississippian period and, I believe, from very much earlier because some of the Mississippian motifs are, in fact, seen earlier in Adena / Hopewell burials:[152] the hand with an eye on the palm, the sun circle, the cross, the raptors, cats, serpents. There are specifically Mississippian motifs, too. Dancing men costumed in elaborate avian regalia, carrying severed heads, appear to be uniquely Mississippian as is the weeping eye motif, the hand-with-cross-on-palm motif, and what Ralph Coe calls a "sun-wind" symbol representing the four directions of the wind (for which he also says a cross may be substituted).[153] I think it possible however that the cross could represent not the four winds so much as the directions east and west, up and down, and only later did it become synonymous with the four winds. James Brown connects the cross-in-circle with "...the solar deity as embodied in the chief"[154] — both scholars again illustrating Eliade's point about multivalent religious symbolism.

A Mississippian temple, dating from 900 CE at Ocmulgee, Georgia, may contain individual vomitoria. There is a recessed basin at every seat. Some scholars speculate a "black drink ceremony" was practiced here.[155] Purgation is a ritual practice of the Creek Indians even today as part of the harvest ceremonies. If so, the numerous Mississippian effigies of male and female figures with protruding tongues may illustrate people vomiting. The figures are a different type than the Mississippian effigy bottles with bared teeth and slitted eyes who are usually thought to be portraits of the dead[156]. Robert Claibourne calls these latter "round-faced caricatures."[157]

Mississippian Burial Ritual

Burial practices at Cahokia are similar to what is known of Adena / Hopewell practice, particularly Hopewell. All graves of whatever type are anointed with red ochre. One excavation, Mound 72 at Cahokia, yielded a mound-within-a-mound with several grouped burials. There were six extended burials, people all buried at the same time, ranging in age from 17-21, half female, half male. Melvin Fowler views this as an example of retainer burial.[158] All have their heads pointed towards Monks Mound,[159] the primary mound in the cluster. One figure is sprawled face down.[160] With these six there was another who was laid to rest on "...more than 10,000 mussel and conch shell beads that had apparently once decorated a cape or blanket."[161] There are at least another 250 burials in the same mound, "...including those of four men with heads and hands removed and a pit containing the bones of more than fifty young women."[162] There are also suggestions that cannibalism may have occurred. Dismembered remains with split long bones have been found in a number of Cahokia excavations, and throughout the upper Great Lakes area.[163] For example, at the Aztalan site (Lake Mills, Wisconsin), the refuse pits contained bundle burials, charred human bones, and many skulls showing "...post mortem removal of large disks."[164] Trepanning, whether of the living or of the dead, is a practice for which evidence has been found in both the New and the Old World from the earliest of times, back even perhaps to the time of the Neanderthal.

The Mississippian Decline

Construction at Cahokia ceased about 1,375 CE for reasons unknown.[165] The area went into a rapid decline. Population pressures were undoubtedly important.[166] Other reasons suggested include epidemics attributed to the Spanish intrusion[167] (DeSoto ravaged the southeast in the 1540s looking for gold); famine due to changes in weather;[168] soil exhaustion;[169] warfare and scalp-collecting.[170] There was a lot of tribal dislocation and transit throughout the middle Mississippi area as people were driven forward by the Iroquois thrust into the valley.[171] So far as is known, the seventeenth-century Iroquois, well settled into the area by the time of European contact, adopted few, if any, of the old Mississippian customs[172] practiced contemporaneously in the southeast.

Whether the pressures came from within or without or from both sides, somewhere about 1,150 CE, stockades were built at Cahokia—inner and outer stockades. The inner stockade was almost 4 m high. Built of 14,000 logs, it had raised platforms every 24 m or so and it was about 3 km long.[173] The dimensions of the outer stockade are not yet known. Monks Mound was at its tallest reach.

Fairly good arguments based on ritual practice and origin myths have been advanced connecting the Creek, Chickashaw, Choctaw, and Cherokee Indians to the Mississippians. For example, the Choctaw believe their ancestors issued forth from a hole in a mound.[174] The Chickashaw believe they came out of the ground[175] someplace west, travelled east to a large river, and built mounds in order to know more about the people on the other side of the river.[176] Was this meant as a devotional act? And for the Cherokee, well into the historic period, the Etowah mound complex, built by the Mississippians years before, was *their ceremonial center*.[177] Even the Tuscarora, an Iroquois-speaking group located in North Carolina, believed that they, too, had their origin in the ground. Sky Holder called them forth.[178] Their origin myth is very different from that of other tribes organized under the Iroquoian League. The difference may be accounted for in part because they are located so much further south than the rest of the league. One suspects an Archaic period carry-over here that transcended the beliefs of the particular language group.

Mesoamerican Influence in Mississippian Earthwork

As we have seen, the discussion of Adena and Hopewell mounds can be overlapped. There are enough contiguous points—shape of mounds, associated earthwork, siting, the motivation for building. Mississippian structures appear so elaborate, baroque, in their conception that the points of contiguity with Adena / Hopewell are obscured by a presumably Mesoamerican style and influence from Mexico. A Mesoamerican influence is certainly there. The mounds are truncated, squared, sequenced platforms with temples or other public structures on top. None of the Adena / Hopewell mounds are like this. Nonetheless, the Mesoamerican influence is laid onto an Adena/Hopewell infrastructure. However predominant the Mississippian temple platform appears on the site, it is there in a necessary conjunction, a coordinate relationship with simpler burial mounds, ossuary structures, and a plaza. As we know, the more sacred something is, the more "holy" in that sense, the more conservative is its display. The burials within the Mississippian burial mound point to the sacred temple shrine, the biggest of the mounds. Its siting in relationship to the plaza orchestrates the siting of all the other mounds in the group.

As for the grandiose size of the Mississippian sacred temple mound? Bigger and better must have been critically important given the population pressures generated by the large Mississippian settlements. How else could one provide for settlements as large as Cahokia in an orderly way? The granaries had to be secured atop platform mounds, and they were. The gods had to be consulted, and they were. Because Monks Mound was so tall, the priest/god dwellers of its summit could look out over the palisade demarcating the sacred area to the four woodhenges, 80m to 145m in diameter, on a cleared plain 1,000 m to the west. There they would see important astronomical alignments[179] just as one could have "read" the alignments of the Poverty Point avenues from the height of the monster-mound itself 2,500 years before.

Purpose of an Earth Interment

Everyone contributed to the effort to maintain or restore order; even the dead so carefully aligned in their earthen mounds had a role to play because death diminished the whole, threatened the group's continuance, interrupted order. When death is viewed in those terms, there is a necessary interconnectedness of the living with the dead. The mound builders chose to inter their dead in the earth. By so doing, they exalted the earth itself (in the form of a mound and its associated earthwork) and asked for pity, for its beneficent intercession, perhaps even for a restoration of life in a new growing form. If the dead were returned to earth, they could be revivified by the earth. What were the siting decisions engendered by such purposeful earth interments?

Endnotes Chapter II

1. John E. Pfeiffer, *The Creative Explosion: An inquiry into the origins of Art and Religion* (New York: Harper & Row, 1982), pp. 114-118.

2. Robert W. Neuman and Nancy W. Hawkins, *Louisiana Prehistory* (Baton Rouge: Louisiana Archaeological Survey and Antiquities Commission Anthropological Study no. 6, 1982), p. 11.

3. William H. Sears, "The Southeastern United States," *Prehistoric Man in the New World*, edited by Jesse David Jennings and Edward Norbeck (Chicago: University of Chicago Press, 1964), p. 260.

4. Jon L. Gibson, *Poverty Point: A Culture of the Lower Mississippi Valley* (Baton Rouge: Louisiana Archaeological Survey and Antiquities Commission Anthropological Study no. 7, 1985), p. 9.

5. *Ibid.*, p. 9.

6. Neuman and Hawkins, *op.cit.*, p. 10.

7. Gibson, op.cit., p. 12.

8. R. S. Newall, *Stonehenge* (London: Her Majesty's Stationery Office, 1959), pp. 20-21.

9. Richard G. Forbis, "Eastern North America" in *North America*, edited by Shirley Gorenstein (New York: St. Martins Press, 1975), p. 84.

10. David S. Brose, James W. Brown, and David W. Penney, *Ancient Art of the American Woodland Indians* (New York: Harry N. Abrams, 1985), p. 183.

11. Gibson, *op.cit., p. 10.*

12. Perhaps the bird identification rests on too strong an association investigators have made between the mound shape (as monster-bird) and a host of very small jasper effigies (called "owl") excavated from the mound and from other Poverty Point culture sites. The shapes of the two are not at all similar. Moreover, no particular importance is attached to the owl by any later mound-building culture elsewhere; whereas, the Poverty Point clam shell effigies, female torso figures, and bird talons do retain their importance for later mound-building cultures. Marija Gimbutas' cautionary tale in *Gods and Goddesses of Old Europe: 7000-3500 BC* (1974), pp. 102-106, regarding the so-called "steatopygous figurines" is worth remembering.

For years archaeologists thought these fleshy, wide-hipped figures an especially grotesque depiction of women because the archaeologists were un-
knowing of the myth of the goddess as bird-about-to-birth-the-cosmic-egg;
hence, the researchers did not understand the neolithic figurines when they
found them. The older a religious idea, the more likely it is to be depicted
in an abstracted, schematized, condensed, composite way. That is why for
every whole animal figure in the paleolithic caves of France and Spain
(Pfeiffer, *op.cit.*, p.140), there are roughly three partial figures and dozens of
abstract forms. The Poverty Point "owl" effigies do not look very owl-like at
all when seen in conjunction with Gimbutas' similarly sized neolithic pillar-
phallic effigies or W. J. Orchard's supposedly paleo-Indian effigies from Sas-
katchewan (*The Stone Age on the Prairies*, 1942). See fig. 9.

13. Neuman and Hawkins, *op.cit.*, p. 11.

14. Gibson, *op.cit.*, pp. 6-7.

15. *Ibid.*, p. 2.

16. *Ibid.*, p. 3.

17. Robert E. Funk, "Post-Pleistocene Adaptations," *Handbook of
North American Indians*, vol. 15: *Northeast* (Washington: Smithsonian Institution, 1978), p. 27.

18. James E. Fitting, "Prehistory: An Introduction," *Handbook of
North American Indians*, vol. 15: *Northeast* (Washington: Smithsonian Institution, 1978), p. 12.

19. James A. Tuck, "Regional Cultural Development, 3000-300 BC,"
Handbook of North American Indians, vol. 15: *Northeast* (Washington:
Smithsonian Institution,1978), p. 43.

20. *Ibid.*; also James B. Griffin in Jennings and Norbeck, p. 235:
"Cremation has been present in the whole Northeast area since about 6000
BC...."

21. Tuck, *op.cit.*, p. 34.

22. Forbis, *op.cit.*, p. 8; Tuck, *loc.cit* p. 34.

23. Tuck, *op.cit.*, pp. 33-34.

24. William A. Ritchie, "Prehistoric Settlement Patterns in Northeastern North America," *Prehistoric Settlement Patterns in the New World*,
edited by Jesse David Jennings and Edward Norbeck (Chicago: University
of Chicago Press, 1964), p. 75.

25. Tuck, *op.cit.*, p. 43.

26. Depending upon the region where these graves are located, this burial cult is variously identified as Maine cemetary complex, Glacial Kame, early Woodlands, Red Ochre, Old Copper, Meadowland, Susquehanna tradition, or Titterington culture.

27. Tuck, *op.cit.*, p. 42.

28. Ritchie, *op.cit.*, p. 74.

29. *Ibid.*

30. Christopher Vecsey, "Introduction," in *American Indian Environment: Ecological Issues in Native American History* (Syracuse: Syracuse University, 1980), edited by Christopher Vecsey and Robert W. Venables, p. xiii; James B. Griffin, "Late Prehistory of the Ohio Valley," *Handbook of North American Indians*, vol.15: *Northeast* (Washington: Smithsonian Institution, 1975), p. 64.

31. Ruth Phillips, personal communication, May 26, 1987.

32. William N. Morgan, *Prehistoric Architecture in the Eastern United States* (Cambridge: The MIT Press, 1980), p. 5.

33. A ring or circle of considerable size might not be too difficult to mark off on cleared land. Three ways come to mind. One person might walk a set number of paces in all directions from a single point. Marking the terminus of each set number of paces would provide a circumference or any part of a circumference desired. Two people connected by a cord (vine, gut, or twisted fiber...) could make a circle if one stood still, and the other rotated about that person at a distance determined by the length of the cord held taut between them. Many people holding hands could also mark out a circumference by rotating as a radius about a point.

34. W. Morgan, *op.cit., p. 5.*

35. *Ibid.*

36. Vecsey, *loc.cit.*

37. Adena takes its name from an estate near Chillicothe, Ohio, where there are some earthworks of that period which were excavated in 1901. Hopewell was similarly named for a man named Hopewell whose Ohio farm with its mounds attracted many amateur archaeologists in the nineteenth century. Mississippian refers, of course, to the Mississippi River.

Along the lower Mississippi are found these later works, which were the first ones known to European explorers.

[38.] Ritchie, *loc.cit.*

[39.] Elman R. Service, *Profiles in Ethnology: A revision of A PROFILE OF PRIMITIVE CULTURE* (New York: Harper & Row, 1963). Bands are hunters, fishers, and gatherers who migrate seasonally, have no formal leaders, no kin obligations. There is communal ownership of subsistence resources, little craft specialization, some inter-band trade. In addition, there is some status differentiation by age and sex, and a shamanic practice of religion. Tribes are farmers, living in villages. There is some sort of political hierarchy, e.g., a tribal council. Rites of theoretical descent are common as are rituals—e.g., counting "coup" or seizing a trophy. There may be cannibalism. Trading networks are extensive. A chiefdom is distinguished by a graded lineage with graded prestige and often a principle of primogeniture. Kinship rankings matter. Sumptuary rules circumscribe the chief's life. The center or capital of the chiefdom will contain the temple, the chief's residence, the storehouses, the priests, and craftsworkers—all of whom work for the greater glory of the chiefdom. Service's schematic description indicates that at the time of European contact (1492), bands were found primarily in Canada, Alaska, the western third of the United States, and the southern third of South America. Religion consisted of life-crisis rites, and shamanic rituals to cure and ensure a food supply. In the Eastern Woodlands, the European explorers found a tribal organization, as in the southwest, and the tropical lowlands of South America and the southern Andes. William T. Sanders and Joseph Marino in their book, *New World Prehistory* (Englewood Cliffs: Prentice-Hall, 1970), pp. 17-20, comment that Service's schematic description—standardly taught in university anthropology courses today—of an evolutionary social progression from band-to-tribe-to-chiefdom is a more appropriate descriptive framework for New World prehistory than the Old World sequence of paleolithic to Bronze Age. Perhaps. But I think Service's description can be fairly questioned even in a New World context. Some important aspects describing prehistoric band structure persist to this day, as do certain of the tribal characteristics identified by Service; whereas, the precontact chiefdom systems are all in disarray. The Old World sequence emphasizes an increasing level of technological sophistication in material culture. Tool making does get better, to a point of acceptable efficiency and aesthetics, but there are always ways to improve a tool. Not so human relationships. The survival of any ancient social structure into our own time should suggest to us that there may be nothing maladaptive, unaccomplished, or simple-minded about it. Nonetheless, the characteristics Service assigns to bands, tribes, and chiefdoms are helpful as descriptors and are the ones I have used—but with an important caveat: I attach no value that one is somehow better than another, nor do I believe an evolutionary progression should be necessarily assumed for tribe-to-chiefdom.

40. Sanders and Marino, *op.cit.*, pp. 95-96: "The archaeological data suggest that agriculture, ceramics, and burial mounds emerged first in the Ohio and middle Mississippi Valley and gradually diffused from that center."

41. Griffin, "The Northeast Woodlands Area," p. 238.

42. Robert Silverberg, *Mound Builders of Ancient America* (Greenwich: New York Graphic Society, 1968), p. 243.

43. *Ibid.*, p. 244.

44. Tuck, *loc. cit.* p. 43.

45. The terms Algonkian, Algonquian, and Algonquin cause much confusion as they are very often used interchangeably. In this study, Algon-**quian** refers to the language group spoken by the Algon**kian** peoples, of whom the Algon**quin** are but one small tribe, now more commonly called the **Ottawa**.

46. Silverberg, *op.cit.*, p.243.

47. Griffin, "The Northeast Woodlands Area," p. 236; Brian Fagan, "Who were the mound builders?" in *Mysteries of the Past*, edited by L. Casson, *et al.* (New York: Simon and Schuster, 1977), p. 121.

48. R. F. Spencer and Jesse David Jennings, *et al.*, *The Native Americans* (New York: Harper & Row, 1977), p. 28; David S. Brose, "The Woodland Period," *Ancient Art of the American Woodland Indians*, ed. David S. Brose, James W. Brown, David W. Penney (New York: Harry N. Abrams, 1985), p. 50.

49. James E. Fitting, "Regional Cultural Development," *Handbook of the North American Indian*, vol. 15: *Northeast* (Washington: Smithsonian Institution, 1978), pp. 44-45.

50. Spencer and Jennings, *op cit*, p. 25: "The highest development in the flowering of the Woodland cultures was in the Ohio-Kentucky area where from 800 BC to AD 600 the Adena-Hopewell cultures centered."

51. *Ibid.*, p.28.

52. Silverberg, *op.cit.*, p. 239.

53. Brose,"The Woodland Period," p. 58.

54. Griffin, "The Northeast Woodlands Area," p. 239.

55. Forbis, *op,cit.*, p. 91; Sanders and Marino, *op.cit.*, p. 96.

56. Fagan, *op.cit.*, p. 127.

57. Forbis, *loc.cit.*, p. 91; Sanders and Marino, *loc.cit.*, p. 96.

58. Fagan, *loc.cit.*, p. 127.

59. Griffin, "The Northeast Woodlands Area," p. 247.

60. Sanders and Marino, *loc.cit.*, p. 96.

61. Griffin, "The Northeast Woodlands Area," p. 242.

62. Silverberg, *op.cit., p. 266.*

63. *Ibid.*, p. 269.

64. *Ibid.*, p. 280.

65. *Ibid.*, p. 280.

66. *Ibid.*, p. 283.

67. *Ibid.*, p. 282.

68. Brose, "The Woodland Period," p. 88.

69. *Ibid.*, p. 88.

70. *Ibid.*, p. 70.

71. *Ibid.*, p. 72.

72. James B. Griffin, "Prehistoric Settlement Patterns in the Northern Mississippi Valley and the Upper Great Lakes", in *Prehistoric Settlement Patterns in the New World*, edited by Gordon R. Willey (New York: Viking Fund, 1956), p. 67.

73. Griffin, "Prehistoric Settlement Patterns," p. 67.

74. W. Sullivan, "Ancient Mounds taken as Clues to Advanced Culture," *The New York Times*, June 19, 1979, p. C3.

75. Joan Vastokas and Romas K. Vastokas, *Sacred Art of the Algonkians* (Peterborough: Mansard, 1973), p. 25.

76. Vastokas and Vastokas, *ibid.*, p. 27.

77. Jesse David Jennings, *Prehistory of North America* (New York: McGraw-Hill Books, 1974), p. 224.

78. Sullivan, *loc.cit.*

79. David I. Bushnell, Jr., *Native Cemeteries and Forms of Burial East of the Mississippi* (Washington: Bureau of American Ethnology, Bulletin 71, 1920), p. 93.

80. Forbis, *op.cit.*, p. 82.

81. Fagan, *op.cit.*, p. 121.

82. Silverberg, *op.cit.*, p. 249.

83. Bushnell, *op.cit.*, pp. 95, 197-198.

84. *Ibid.*, pp. 73-74.

85. Fagan, *op.cit.*, p. 120.

86. Jennings, *Prehistory of North America*, p. 226.

87. Silverberg, *op.cit.*, p. 254.

88. *Ibid.*, p. 280.

89. Bushnell, *op.cit.*, p. 64.

90. Fitting, "Regional Cultural Development," p. 45.

91. Griffin, "The Northeast Woodlands Area," p. 247.

92. Silverberg, *op.cit.*, p. 247.

93. Ella Elizabeth Clark, *Indian Legends of Canada* (Toronto: McClelland and Stewart, Ltd., 1960), pp. 1-4.

94. Spencer and Jennings, *op.cit.*, p. 25.

95. Ralph T. Coe, *Sacred Circles: Two thousand years of North American Indian art* (London: Art Council of Great Britain, 1976), p. 54.

96. Fagan, *op.cit.*, p.121.

[97.] Jennings, *Prehistory of North America*, p. 226.

[98.] Griffin, "Prehistoric Settlement Patterns," p. 68.

[99.] Fitting, "Regional Cultural Development," p. 53.

[100.] Spencer and Jennings, *op.cit.*, p. 27.

[101.] Robert Claibourne, *The Emergence of Man: The first Americans* (New York: Time-Life Books, 1973), p. 131.

[102.] Griffin, "Prehistoric Settlement Patterns," p. 67.

[103.] Silverberg, *op.cit.*, p. 283; Claibourne, *op.cit.*, p. 132.

[104.] Forbis, *op.cit.*, p. 90; Fitting, "Regional Cultural Development," p. 48.

[105.] Sanders and Marino, *op.cit.*, p. 98.

[106.] Fagan, *op.cit.*, p. 133.

[107.] Griffin, "The Northeast Woodlands Area," p. 248.

[108.] Forbis, *op.cit.*, p. 94.

[109.] Griffin, "The Northeast Woodlands Area," p. 248; Forbis, *op.cit.*, p. 100.

[110.] Fagan, *loc.cit.*

[111.] Sanders and Marino, *op.cit.*, p. 97.

[112.] James A. Brown, "The Mississippian Period," *Ancient Art of the American Woodland Indians,* ed. by David S. Brose, James A. Brown, David W. Penney (New York: Harry N. Abrams, 1985), p. 96.

[113.] *Ibid.*, p. 97.

[114.] *Ibid.*

[115.] William H. Sears, however, makes a case for the reverse: "I do not know where, or precisely from what, this culture originated. The general area of origin is certainly north of the Mason-Dixon line in the great flat bottomlands of the Mississippi and the lower Ohio, Illinois, and Tennessee rivers.. . ." in "The Southeastern United States," *Prehistoric Man in the New World,* edited by Jesse David Jennings and Edward Norbeck (Chicago: University of Chicago Press, 1964), p. 277.

116. Morgan, *op.cit.,* p. 58.

117. James B. Griffin, "Late Prehistory of the Ohio Valley," *Handbook of the North American Indians,* vol. 15: *Northeast* (Washington: Smithsonian Institution, 1975), p. 548.

118. *Ibid.*

119. Nelson A. Reed, "Monks and other Mississippian Mounds" in *Explorations into Cahokia Archaeology,* edited by Melvin L. Fowler (Urbana: University of Illinois, 1973), p. 37.

120. John Pfeiffer, "America's First City," *Horizons,* Spring 1974, pp. 59-63.

121. Griffin, "Prehistoric Settlement Patterns," p. 71.

122. Forbis, *op.cit.,* p. 95.

123. Griffin, "Prehistoric Settlement Patterns," p. 71; Sanders and Marino, *op.cit.,* p. 97.

124. James A. Brown, *loc.cit.* p. 96.

125. Reed, *op.cit.,* p. 31.

126. *Ibid.*

127. Melvin L. Fowler and Robert L. Hall, "Late Prehistory of the Illinois Area," *Handbook of North American Indians,* vol. 15: *Northeast* (Washington: Smithsonian Institution, 1975), p. 567; Reed, *op.cit.,* p. 39.

120. James A. Brown, *loc.cit.*

129. E. Shrum, "Meet the Mound Builders," *Hobbies,* June 1983, pp. 12 ff.

130. Griffin, "The Northeast Woodlands Area," p. 249.

131. Fowler and Hall, *op.cit.,* p. 560.

132. Sanders and Marino, *op.cit.,* p. 97.

133. Fowler and Hall, *loc.cit.*

134. Forbis, *op.cit.*, p. 98.

135. Shrum, *op.cit.*, p. 73.

136. Griffin, "The Northeast Woodlands Area," p. 249; Fowler and Hall, *op.cit.*, p. 567.

137. Sanders and Marino, *loc.cit.*

138. Sears, *op.cit.*, p. 278; Forbis, *op.cit.*, p. 96; Ralph T. Coe, *op.cit.*, p. 57; Silverberg, *op.cit.*, p. 316.

139. James A. Brown, "The Mississippian Period," p. 103.

140. Griffin, "The Northeast Woodlands Area," p. 249

141. James A. Brown, "The Mississippian Period," pp. 104-105.

142. Reed, *op.cit.*, p. 39.

143. Mircea Eliade, "Methodological Remarks on the Study of Religious Symbolism," *The History of Religions: Essays in Methodology*, edited by Mircea Eliade and Joseph Kitagawa (Chicago: University of Chicago Press, 1959), p. 99.

144. *Ibid.*

145. Åke Hultkrantz, *Prairie and Plains Indians* (Leiden: E. J. Brill, 1973), p. 2.

146. *Ibid.*, p. 3.

147. *Ibid.*, p. 5.

148. *Ibid.*, p. 7.

149. *Ibid.*, p. 19.

150. *Ibid.*, p. 21.

151. James A. Brown, "The Mississippian Period," p. 106.

152. Forbis, *op.cit.*, p. 96.

153. Ralph T. Coe, *op.cit.*, p. 15.

154. James A. Brown, "The Mississippian Period," p. 111.

155. Silverberg, *op.cit.*, pp. 303-304.

156. Brose, "The Woodland Period," p. 77.

157. Claibourne, *op.cit.*, p. 135.

158. Melvin L. Fowler, "The Cahokia Site," *Explorations into Cahokia Archaeology* (Urbana: University of Illinois, 1973), p. 19.

159. Fowler and Hall, *op.cit.*, p. 565.

160. Pfeiffer, *op.cit.*, pp. 59-63.

161. *Ibid.*

162. *Ibid.*

163. David S. Brose, "Late Prehistory of the Upper Great Lakes Area," *Handbook of North American Indians*, vol. 15: *Northeast* (Washington: Smithsonian Institution, 1975), pp. 571-580.

164. Brose, "Late Prehistory," p. 573.

165. Shrum, *op.cit.*, p. 74.

166. Pfeiffer, *loc.cit.*

167. Sears, *op.cit.*, p. 283; Shrum, *op.cit.*, p. 75; Fowler and Hall, *op.cit.*, p. 568.

168. Shrum, *loc.cit.*

169. Griffin, "The Northeast Woodlands Area," p. 254. For example: "Historical records show that some Iroquois groups moved their main village about every 10 years because of soil and firewood depletion, and archaeological work in New York State tends to substantiate this behavior for late prehistoric times."

170. Silverberg, *op.cit.*, p. 326.

171. Fowler and Hall, *op.cit.*, p. 568.

172. Forbis, *op.cit.*, p. 96.

173. Pfeiffer, *loc.cit.*

174. Ralph T. Coe, *op.cit.*, p. 54.

175. Silverberg, *op.cit.*, p. 327.

176. *Ibid.*

177. Sears, *op.cit.*, p. 281.

178. Clark, *op.cit.*, pp. 3-4.

179. Warren L. Wittry, "An American Woodhenge," in *Native North American Art History: Selected Readings*, edited by Zena Pearlstone Mathews and Aldona Jonaitis (Palo Alto: Peek Publications, 1982), pp. 454-455.

Chapter III

SITE ORIENTATION FACTORS

In the previous chapter the mound was described as an architectural form in the sense that it is useful to know what mounds look like, what was placed within, why, and who were the people who built them. When we look at any building today, those are just the sort of questions we are asking when we say: and ask: "What is that building over there?" We expect answers along functional lines: what is the *use* of the building, what goes on inside it, and why, and for whose benefit. In the case of the mound builders, we know they piled earth high as places of interment and, sometimes, as places of observation for movements of the heavens. We do not know much more.

The chapter also reviewed, in very general terms, what is known anthropologically about the Mississippi Valley mound-building peoples and suggested a continuity of motivation in all mound-building activity, wherever it occurs. The interments are sacred because bodies and bones preserved and burnished with red ochre are returned to earth. The astronomical movements are important because they are indicators of order. The arrangement of objects within the mounds is orderly and purposeful. The construction of the mound itself and its associated earthwork is a purposeful activity. It matters what site is selected because the earth mound has the potential of being an animating agent, of repairing the rupture caused by death, if all is done properly. This leads us into a discussion of siting factors.

Siting Decisions

It is usual to think of architectural forms as either site-adapted or site-imposed. If site-imposed, like the pyramids at Giza, the forms can be put down anywhere and will have a similar effect because their relationship is one to the other. A site-imposed architectural work is more likely to exhibit right angles, parallel lines, and cardinal point orientation. Its relationship to a land feature — a ridge, a watercourse, a plain or valley, a "view" — is secondary, often distinctly secondary, at least to a modern eye. Our contemporary International-style skyscrapers are site-imposed works. That is why modern cities have a similar look about them anywhere, no matter the climate, the terrain. Brasilia might have been New Delhi, viewed as an architectural drawing, that is.

Site-adapted architecture seems to "blend" more with the landscape, to be necessarily related to some feature of the terrain, of a "natural" trees-and-water landscape, usually. Very often the "view" is primary and obvious because it is the intent of the architect to "frame" the view. Site-adapted architecture is specific to its location; landscape features are the preeminent siting factors. Douglas J. Cardinal's undulating forms for Ottawa's new Canadian Museum of Civilization is a classic example of the concerns of site-adapted architecture: the landscape is enhanced.

Unlike the pyramids, Stonehenge, or the Great Wall of China, Amerindian mounds have been little dealt with as works in and of themselves. They are confusing, their arrangement perplexing. Yet even in dismal black and white photography, the mounds appeal to modern sensibilities for reasons almost inchoate. One of Martha Graham's most important dance works, *Rite of Spring*, was inspired by no more than an aerial photograph of the Great Serpent Mound (Peebles, Ohio).[1] (See fig. 16.)

Caleb Atwater and others surveyed some of the mounds in the first half of the nineteenth century. But not until 1848 was a comprehensive survey of the Mississippi valley mounds published: *Ancient Monuments of the Mississippi Valley: Comprising the Results of Extensive Original Surveys and Explorations* by E. G. Squier and E. H. Davis, the first volume of the *Smithsonian Contributions to Knowledge*. Another comprehensive survey would not be published again until 1980 — *Prehistoric Architecture in the Eastern United States* by William N. Morgan. It is interesting to compare the findings of these two works for several reasons: First, as already mentioned, for all the attention given to the artifacts themselves, little has been directed to the mounds and their associated earthworks as purposeful compositions in and of themselves. This is an error because the siting decisions for so large a sequence of endeavors over such a long stretch of time did not "just happen." Second, what little has been written about siting is contradictory and confusing. For example: Nelson A. Reed reviewed 131 Mississippian sites (as reported in his too-short 1973 paper) to see if he could discern an orientation factor for the principle mound. He concluded orientation was random because the mounds were sited in "relationship to the plaza and the surrounding environment."[2] Had he spelled out what were the significant factors in the surrounding environment, one would then have an orientation factor *specific, not random.* Like Reed, Morgan found no particular direction operative in his resurveying of the sites, but he did think the structures more site-adapted than site-imposed and that there might be some relationship to the land at work in the siting decisions taken.[3] Unfortunately, Morgan, too, never spelled out what this relationship of site to structure might be. Given that Vincent Scully's study of the Greek temple and its relationship to distant views (*Earth, Temple, and the Gods*, 1962) is such a well-known thesis, one is surprised neither Morgan nor Reed looked further afield for a site-orientation factor. Squier, however, apparently did. For him, there are physical characteristics which indicate what earthworks are religious and what ones are not (he calls the latter structures "defensive"). Religious structures are those having a cleared plain about them, interior ditches, and an easterly orientation.

All three men looked at a number of the same sites, albeit one was on the scene over a hundred years earlier. Perhaps Morgan and Reed were hampered by their considerable technical proficiency. Morgan is an architect; Reed is an archaeologist. They appear to have looked for pinpoint cardinal precision. Finding none, they did not say there was *no* directional orientation, they do hint perhaps there might be *something*: perhaps the work might be site-adapted, not site-imposed. (In fact, the chances are pretty good given the current progress of archaeoastronomy studies in the United States that part of the "something" will be solstice alignments.)[4] Squier, on the other hand, had no particular expertise to bring to his study of the mounds. He was only a newspaper editor in Ohio when he began his Sunday afternoon strolls out along the greensward.[5]

Monks Mound and Others

Nelson Reed's study starts with Monks Mound as its jumping-off point. Monks Mound is a multiple-terraced mound having both an east-west axis and a north-south axis. It originally faced a plaza on the east, an orientation later changed to the south. It is the principal mound determining the orientation for all other mounds at Cahokia. Reed's study was set up to determine if those things were so elsewhere for other Mississippian sites. Somehow, Reed managed to conclude they were not. He did find that mounds in clusters are arranged at right angles or are parallel to one another in relationship to the principal mound (just as at Cahokia). He stated he found no particular "celestial pattern" in the orientation of the principal mound. Reed noted that the principal mound is usually west of its plaza, but seems to be there with "...no cardinal precision."[6] He concluded it is probably the plaza itself which determines the orientation of the mound, and the plaza is laid out in relationship to a "...river, slough, or ridge."[7] In other words, the principal mound looks out roughly east over a plaza that commands a river view. This view (the river, slough, or ridge) is the most important feature of the siting.

Is this observation true for the Adena and Hopewell sites surveyed by Morgan and Squier? What about the other sites in Morgan's study, the Mississippian sites?

In a word, "no."

Yes, there is often a river view (or slough, or ridge). But no, it is not the most important factor determining the siting decision. Something else is taken into account—an easterly direction. Almost always it is the more important factor. In fact, the original east-west orientation of Monks Mound itself bears this out. The watercourses available as views were north and south of the mound. They only became views when the mound was reoriented.

In his study, *Prehistoric Architecture in the Eastern United States*, Morgan selected 82 sites for study, mostly built between 1,000 BCE and 1,500 CE. His selection is a comprehensive sampling of more than 400 sites still available for study at the time of his survey. His final selection was based on several criteria, not the least of which was a desire to show geographical and chronological diversity. There is an emphasis on selection of mound sites where mounds are displayed in groups.[8]

Thus, the selection available for study in his text will serve our purposes well enough to review the problem of siting vis-à-vis water and celestial directionality.

Archaic Site Orientation

Morgan's study includes three archaic sites: Sapelo, Fig Island, and Poverty Point. All three are oriented in an easterly fashion if one understands easterly to be the opening of a circle in any northeast, east, or southeast direction, or the lowest side of a shell embankment. In one case, Poverty Point, the concentric arcs open east in direct alignment to the waterfront (see fig. 17, also 7, 8). In another case, Edisto Island, the waterfront is to the west and the ring opening is northeast (see fig. 10). And in the third, Sapelo (see fig. 18), all three of the shell rings are closed and scattered, so no sense of alignment can be drawn, although the watercourse is to the west.

Adena / Hopewell Site Orientation

Of the 23 Adena / Hopewell sites in Morgan's text,[9] two are effigy figures and considered in this paper for directional factors, and two are features of the same site. They are thus considered as one site. Of the 20 remaining sites, waterfront relationships are shown for 18. Of these 18, alignment to a specific land feature appears to have established the directionality of the earthwork only four times: Twice the earthwork was oriented east to water—Marksville and Tchula Lake (see figs. 19, 20). Twice the earthwork's north-south orientation was paralleled by the waterfront itself running north-south to the west—Stone Work and Seal (see figs. 21, 22).

The most desirable location does appear to be water east of the earthwork, and a straight-on east directionalism for the earthwork itself. In addition to the two times that actually does happen, there are five more times where the watercourse was northeast or southeast of a work having an easterly orientation. All together then, seven times water and the earthwork are in rough alignment to one another, and the alignment is easterly. The importance of this easterly orientation in the Adena / Hopewell earthwork is further demonstrated by the eight times water runs west, or south, or northwest of the earthwork, and is not a prime directional siting factor. The earthwork in such cases is always sited easterly. Apparently, too, no site in this small sample having water due north was ever selected.

Mississippian Site Orientation

Of the 57 Mississippian sites,[10] all but six have waterfronts shown on their site drawings. One is a composite Adena-Hopewell-Mississippian site (see fig. 23). Of these 51, only three earthworks are not arranged in an easterly direction. They appear to be situations where the location of the waterfront was, indeed, the primary siting factor: Two face north towards water to the north—Lake George (see fig. 24) and Lake Jackson. The third faces north, but water is to the south—Mount Royal. The later additions to Monks Mound at Cahokia reorient it to a north-south axis, facing south, and watercourses both north and south. The southern one is much the larger. Still, it was originally oriented east.

Of the six where no waterfront is shown at all, Alphenia is one example (see fig. 25). Alphenia is an arrangement of four truncated pyramids on the east bank of the Tensa River. According to Morgan, Alphenia "...was placed on a four-sided plain that was biaxially symmetrical about an 80-meter square plaza oriented to the cardinal points."[11] Such site imposition seems unusual, even for a Mississippian complex.

Of the 39 other sites, all with earthwork in an easterly direction, 18 are sited with a waterfront to the east, two with water to the southeast, and three with water to the northeast for a total of 23. The strong suspicion in the smaller Adena / Hopewell group of Morgan's text that the most auspicious site was one with water east seems to be borne out here in this second sample, too, from Morgan's study.

Nine of the Mississippian sites in Morgan are ringed by water and have an easterly direction. This may be the most favourable of all situations. It is surely the most special—to build on a promontory facing east (see fig. 26), or in the curve of an oxbow, or in a surround of water.

Easterliness plus surround provides us with a composite picture that 32 of the 51 sites favoured an eastern orientation for both earthwork and water. No other water direction is even a close second: south occurs six times; west six times; southwest once; north three times.

For the most part, the easterly direction of the Mississippian sites in Morgan is determined by observing the approach of the ramp up the side of the principal mound. If it is on the west or the east, it is always possible then upon reaching the top to look out directly over a clear expanse to the east. Look straight ahead or turnabout 180 degrees. Just as the Adena / Hopewell sites in the previous sample from Morgan demonstrate, east may be east, southeast, or northeast. The intention of the orientation is the same.

We have here then a special case of site adaptation in mound architecture: water is important; more important is the view to the east. There is, in fact, a consistent easterly directionality in the arrangement of the earthwork itself about the plain in Adena / Hopewell and Mississippian sites.

The Sunwise Direction

Why should our line of vision, our physical movement about the site, the order in which we see and understand things on the site, be directed east? To acknowledge the rising of the sun, always the direction most sacred from the earliest of times.

E. G. Squier noted this general easterly characteristic in mound siting more than a hundred years earlier in the Ohio Valley. Trusting his sense of observation, he was sure the Scioto Valley's circle and square enclosures were what he called "...'tabooed' or consecrated ground."[12] Squier described the circles in this manner: "The greater number of the circles are of small size, with a nearly uniform diameter of two hundred and fifty or three hundred feet, and invariably have the ditch interior to the wall. These have always a single gateway, opening oftenest to the east, though by no means observing a fixed rule in that respect."[13]

Commenting on the extraordinary length and complexity of the parallels often accompanying the circles and squares (see fig. 11), Squier in a notable flash of intuition wrote: "We can find their parallels only in the great temples of Abury and Stonehenge in England, and Carnac in Brittany, and must associate them with sun worship, and its kindred superstitions."[14]

That is a reasonable association to make. As with the Adena/Hopewell earthworks and mounds, in neolithic Great Britain, too, all of the henges are not only roughly circular, but they also have an interior ditch and only one or two entrances.[15] Furthermore, the usual configuration of a British "causewayed camp" — at least in the Wessex area — was that it have an internal area "...of which little is known, surrounded by up to three interrupted concentric ditches with banks on their inner side."[16]

Again, not unlike an Adena/Hopewell earthwork such as those in Portsmouth (see fig. 11).

Like Squier, Morgan, too, was drawn to make a number of provocative comparisons between the New World and the Old. Unlike Squier, however, Morgan's Old World comparisons are not just archaeological, but also psychological. Morgan presents the use of space as a mind-set and concludes his examination of the Amerindian mound sites with parallel illustrations drawn from Stonehenge, Telleborg, the pyramids at Giza, the Acropolis, plus Angkor Wat, the Piazza San Marco, and others.

Both men are right.

Old World Neolithic Practice

There are provocative parallels to be drawn—psychological, religious, and archaeological—between earthwork of the New World and that of the Old. Although it is not my intention to examine such parallels in any detail, a few are presented as illustrative examples in order to help the reader understand that the ancient Amerindian forms properly belong in any discussion about neolithic religious practice. Amerindian material is too often omitted. The general historical framework most of us have for organizing historical data is one which presents Western civilization as having sprung into being in Mesopotamia, then marching forward relentlessly into its millennial New World reckoning. The difficulty with this framework is that it presumes nothing historically interesting was happening elsewhere. The reader's attention, therefore, is drawn briefly to archaic burial practices in Denmark that are roughly, very roughly, contemporaneous with archaic Amerindian practices, particularly concerning mound construction. The Danish material makes a useful comparison because it is well documented and its iconographical meaning understood and accepted, but any neolithic grouping anywhere might have served to demonstrate how a mound, properly sited, becomes an archetypal solution to the problem death presents to an archaic community—"archetype" in an Eliadean, not a Jungean mode.[17]

About 3,000 BCE the first dolmens in Denmark were erected, each with a grave within, the capstone supported by three, four, five, or six stones, usually three (see fig. 27). This was about the same time that the paleo-Indian population in North America exploded, leaving Archaic grave sites with red ochre anointment and grave goods from one end of the continent to the other, but no dolmen burials. There are none in North

America. However, some medicine wheels do have rock cairns containing individual interments. These would be very old, older than the Danish dolmens. Palle Lauring suggests that the Danish dolmens are really better understood as shrines, not graves — so, too, medicine wheels — because the capstone itself could be "...venerated as a potent and sacred object."[18] It always protruded above the ground. The supporting stones and the body within were covered by earth. If the dolmen is a shrine, then the purpose of the body within is to add power to the capstone.[19] The custom of adding a (usually living) body to the foundation of a sacred construction is one found worldwide — whether it be Stonehenge, the northwest coast of Canada, or the South Seas.

There were other sorts of ancient ways to use stone in North American graves. One type practiced all over the continent during the Archaic period was burial in a flexed position with a heavy stone slab, or metate, placed on top of the corpse, then an earth covering. Connections between this practice and the later Amerindian development of the stone cist grave and the mound seem clear.

In Denmark, a thousand years later, low burial mounds and individual stone cists were painstakingly built. Burial mounds and stone cists were certainly common enough practices in North America, too. By the end of the Bronze Age in Denmark, around 1,000 BCE, burial mounds were now piled high, tall structures 15 m to 25 m (see fig. 28), just as in the Mississippi delta at the same time (Poverty Point); however, burial mounds continued to be built for a much longer period of time in North America than in Denmark.

About 2,000 BCE, passage graves were also widely constructed in Denmark. These are T-shaped passages, stone-faced, often entered by crawling on all fours, and completely covered with earth. Of all the stonework construction, the passage grave was probably the most difficult to build, given the tools at hand, which included fire and water to split the stone — thus, no doubt, doubly reinforcing the interment site's sacramental meaning. All were built in Denmark within only one or two generations. None are known in North America, but caves one crawled into were frequent sites of Archaic period basket burials. Moreover, it is easy to associate fire and water, along with stone or earth, with Amerindian grave construction methods at any time historically or pre-contact.

There were hundreds of entombments in some of the Danish passage graves despite their having been used for only a few generations. All of the burials were women and their children; all were female devotees of the mother goddess,[20] whose symbols were found in the crypts.[21] Although almost every historically known activity in Amerindian life is sex-differentiated, no matter the tribal group considered (and we must assume it was so in pre-contact times), no particular separation of the sexes has ever been required in Amerindian burials, only in the burial rituals. It is usually the Amerindian woman who prepares the body for burial, constructs the burial site, and performs the burial devotions.

In Denmark, passage grave construction and use ceased quickly because Denmark was invaded by another group of people who were not devotees of the mother goddess. They were builders of burial mounds.[22] At first the invaders practiced an inhumation of both men and women, laying their bodies together along an east-west axis,[23] mimicking the "sunwise" route of the rising sun throughout the day. But by 1,000 BCE cremation had become the dominant practice in Denmark.[24]

In Denmark, as in North America, there seems to be a status differentiation associated with cremation. One can imagine cremation serving as a holding action until the opportunity arose for interring the remains with a really important or wealthy personage for whom a status mound was to be constructed. This would explain the status differentiation evident within the mound. Not all mound cremations need have been "retainer burials," as anthropologists generally assume, no matter when or where they are found.

P. V. Glob interprets the rapid changeover from inhumation to cremation in Denmark to mean: "The dead no longer had their dwelling place in the burial mounds but instead the soul was freed from the body with the help of fire, and flew to the distant land of the dead where it was reborn."[25] Glob credits this to "...a complete revolution in religious ideas ushering in the period we call the Late Bronze Age."[26] I agree. There is no other reason that would be so persuasive so rapidly.

Cremation never replaced inhumation in ancient Amerindian burial custom. There was always some sort of return to the earth needed until well into the historic period when the Plains people began leaving bodies exposed and elevated on platforms or in trees. There was no later interment of the remains.

Danish cremations often included birds, scores of birds along with the person. Glob believes the intention was to provide the human soul with wing power to bear it to the land of the dead.[27] Since Archaic times, birds have been found in Amerindian grave sites and medicine bundles. The meaning is not clearly specified, but the Hopewell motif of the falcon has been connected with the practice of exposing bodies for a period of time before cremation. This enables raptorial birds, such as the falcon, to strip the bones of their flesh.

Cremated remains were always inserted into Danish burial mounds on the east or south side: "The north side was avoided all together (sic). This was the shadow side, where the sun's rays hardly penetrated, where darkness brooded."[28] The same practice existed in Amerindian mound interment; and, as we have seen earlier in this section, the preferred orientation of an Amerindian mound was easterly—the rising sun warming and renewing the earth and all it contains.

East, the Sacred Direction

East, the sacred direction, is equivalent to the rising sun. One suspects the intention of an east-oriented earth interment is to warm the bones, to renew, to revivify the remains. But what does all that really mean? The above statements, however pretty, are a thin, weak gruel.

I am arguing here for an understanding of mound building as a sacred activity whose meaning is found in the intentional decisions taken to build a mound and its associated earthwork. My argument is largely a historical one, yet one that quite specifically points to east as the preeminent Amerindian siting factor decision. The argument assumes death is disruptive. If so, there is a strong motivation to restore order. Right and proper burials are helpful; so, too, right and proper movements of the sun. Thus, burial mounds are carefully built with an easterly orientation, facing the sunrise, and the solstices sought out.

For a very long time, people have placed their dead in earthen mounds oriented east. The mound, found worldwide, and used in the same or similar way, is certainly an archetype. All attempts to understand archetypes—the quintessential, multivalent religious symbol—start with myth because, as Mircea Eliade argues, in archaic and primitive societies, the myth is what is really real.[29] If we are to make a meal of this thin conjectural gruel, its nourishment will come from myth. Have we any basis there for assuming east equivalent to the rising sun as also meaning renewal, re-creation?

Endnotes Chapter III.

1. Anna Kisselgoff, "The Ancient Relationship of Goddesses and the Dance," *The New York Times*, December 14, 1986, p. H-18: "We all know Miss Graham is up on her snake goddesses, but perhaps her usual multi-level richness was missed by those who did not understand the associations she brought to the climax of her 'Rite.'"

2. Nelson A. Reed, "Monks and other Mississippian Mounds," *Explorations into Cahokia Archaeology*, edited by Melvin L. Fowler (Urbana: University of Illinois, 1973), p. 35.

3. William N. Morgan, *Prehistoric Architecture in the Eastern United States* (Cambridge: The MIT Press, 1980), p. xxvii.

4. Several American archaeologists are working in this area and having a fair amount of preliminary success sorting out suspected astronomical alignments. To my knowledge, they include: Martha Rolingson, Ph.D., (Arkansas Archaeological Survey); Patricia Essenpreis, Ph.D., (University of Florida); Martha Otto, Ph.D., (Ohio Historical Society); and N-omi Greber, Ph.D., (Cleveland Museum of Natural History).

5. Newspaper editors are not an inconclusive breed, nor was Squier. He left newspaper work to run for public office, served several terms in the Ohio Legislature, became a national figure when his mound survey was published, and went on to a diplomatic career as a presidentially appointed ambassador in Central America.

6. Reed, *op.cit.*, p. 40.

7. *Ibid.*, p. 35.

8. William N. Morgan, *op.cit.*, p. xi.

9. Bainbridge (Bainbridge, Ohio); Cedar Bank (Chillicothe, Ohio); Crystal River (Crystal River, Florida); Dublin (Dublin, Ohio); Fort Center (Lakeport, Florida); Graded Way (Piketon, Ohio); High Bank (Chillicothe, Ohio); Kanawha (Charleston, West Virginia); Lizard (West Bend, Wisconsin); Marietta (Marietta, Ohio); Marksville (Marksville, Louisiana); Newark (Newark, Ohio); New Castle (New Castle, Indiana); Oldtown (Frankfort, Ohio); Pinson (Pinson, Tennessee); Portsmouth "C" (Greenup, Kentucky); Seal (Piketon, Ohio); Serpent Mound (Peebles, Ohio); Spanish Fort (Holly Bluff, Mississippi); Stone Work (Chillicothe, Ohio); South Charleston (South Charleston, West Virginia); Tchula Lake (Tchula, Mississippi); and Tick Island(Astor, Florida).

10. Alligator (Bobo, Mississippi); Alphenia (Clayton, Louisiana); Angel (Evansville, Indiana); Anna (Natchez, Mississippi); Arcola (Arcola, Mississippi); Aztalan (Lake Mills, Wisconsin); Barney (Helena, Arkansas); Beckwith's Fort (East Prairie, Missouri); Big Mound City (Indiantown, Florida); Big Tonys (Clewiston, Florida); Cahokia (Collinsville, Illinois); Chucalissa (Memphis, Tennessee); Emerald (Stanton, Mississippi); Etowah (Cartersville, Georgia); Fatherland (Natchez, Mississippi); Fitzhugh (Mound, Louisiana); Greenhouse (Marksville, Louisiana); Haynes Bluff (Haynes Bluff Landing, Mississippi); Hiwassee (Dayton, Tennessee); Irene (Savannah, Georgia); Jackson Place (Floyd, Louisiana); Jerden (Oak Ridge, Louisiana); Kincaid (Brockport, Illinois); Kinlock (Tralake, Mississippi); Kolomoki (Blakely, Georgia); Lake George (Holly Bluff, Mississippi); Lake Jackson (Tallahassee, Florida); Lenoir (Lenoir City, Tennessee); Lilbourn (Lilbourn, Missouri); Lindsley (Lebanon, Tennessee); Long Key (St. Petersbury Beach, Florida); Magee (Percy, Mississippi); Marietta (Marietta, Ohio); Mayersville (Mayersville, Mississippi); Menard (Arkansas Post, Arkansas); Mineral Springs (Mineral Springs, Arkansas); Mott (Lamar, Louisiana); Mound Bottom (Kingston Springs, Tennessee); Moundville (Moundville, Alabama); Mount Royal (Welaka, Florida); Obion (Paris, Tennessee); Ocmulgee (Macon, Georgia); Parkin (Parkin, Arkansas); Perkins (Scott, Mississippi); Philip (Marion Haven, Florida); Sherman (Osceola, Arkansas); Shields (Jacksonville, Florida); Shiloh (Pittsburgh Landing, Tennessee); Spiro (Spiro, Oklahoma); St. Louis (St. Louis, Missouri); Terra Ceia (Bradenton, Florida); Toltec (Little Rock, Arkansas); Town Creek (Mt. Gilead, North Carolina); Troyville (Troyville, Louisiana); Turtle (New Smyrna Beach, Florida); Upper Nodena (Wilson, Arkansas); and Winterville (Greenville, Mississippi).

11. Morgan, *op.cit.*, p. 98.

12. E. G. Squier and E. H. Davis, *Ancient Monuments of the Mississippi Valley: Comprising the results of the extensive original surveys and explorations* (Washington: Smithsonian Contributions to Knowledge, vol. 1, 1848), p. 47.

13. *Ibid.*, p. 48.

14. *Ibid.*, p. 49.

15. Richard Wainwright, *Prehistoric Remains in Britain*, vol. 1, (London: Constable, 1978), p. 21.

16. *Ibid.*, p. 19.

17. As Mircea Eliade explains so often, an archetype is a paradigm, an exemplary model, a reality understood in myth, a symbol resistant to time,

inherently contradictory, yet consistent. It is, of course, related to Jung's sense of the archetype.

[18.] Palle Lauring, *Land of the Tollund Man: The prehistory and archaeology of Denmark* (New York: Macmillan, 1958), p. 52.

[19.] *Ibid.*

[20.] Peter Vilhelm Glob, *Denmark: An archaeological history from the Stone Age to the Vikings* (Ithaca: Cornell University Press, 1971), p. 99.

[21.] *Ibid.*, P. 100.

[22.] *Ibid.*, P. 101.

[23.] *Ibid.*, P. 103.

[24.] *Ibid.*, P. 139.

[25.] *Ibid.*, P. 139.

[26.] *Ibid.*, P. 139.

[27.] *Ibid.*, P. 139: "We cannot doubt the intention behind the layering of so many wings on the pyre along with the dead: the twelve small wings and four large ones were to bear the soul safely to the Land of the Dead."

[28.] *Ibid.*, p. 140.

[29.] Unfortunately, it is not so for us. The process of de-mythologizing in Western society began long ago in archaic Greece, according to Mircea Eliade, *Myth and Reality*, pp. 1-2, (New York: Harper & Row, 1963), when Xenophanes criticized Homer's account of the Trojan War as false: "...the Greeks steadily continued to empty mythos of all religious and metaphysical value. Contrasted with both logos and, later, with historia, mythos came in the end to denote 'what cannot really exist.' On its side Judaeo-Christianity put the stamp of 'falsehood' and 'illusion' on whatever was not justified or validated by the two Testaments." We have not been the same since. In North America, 1492 is the beginning of the end of "really real" mythos. Fortunately, Amerindian myth has withstood well enough many European attempts to undermine it. It still rings true — even to a Western ear.

Chapter IV

A SACRED DIRECTION IN MYTH

Since the time of the paleo-Indian, the eastern directional referent in space direction has been the most important land siting direction. Can a case be made for east as a sacred direction?

Yes. Because sunwise, east, is the sacred direction pre-eminently and consistently today in Amerindian religious ritual,[1] one may expect east to be pre-eminent in Amerindian religious ritual long ago. One approach then would be to determine if there is any demonstration of concern for directionality in Amerindian myth. And if so, what direction? Is it, after all, east? And what is its contextual meaning within the myth?

The answers can be sought within recorded Amerindian myth. for a religious historian these are "the" primary documents, although their value is often discounted. The usual criticisms are several: We tend to assume that stories recorded in the earliest contact days are suspect because they were not *properly* (i.e., ethnographically) set down; we also tend to assume that stories more recently collected are miserably contaminated by Christianizing influence; and, worse yet, we are sometimes asked to wonder if the person telling the story was *really* qualified to speak of such sacred things. I think we can get ourselves out this thicket of assumptions by simply presuming there is a continuity of mythic content—no matter how a story is recorded or collected. That assumption is probably trustworthy on two counts. Many aspects of traditional life among the Amerindian peoples persist today as much because of the isolation of native peoples from mainstream North American culture as because of the continuing botched efforts of outsiders to "educate" native peoples. Further, as John E. Pfeiffer notes when a society is shifting from non-print to print literary, the stories

recorded at the time of that shift ". . . tend to be closely related to last poeti-
cally transmitted myths of its nonliterate days."[2]

The Persistent Significance of Myth

Mythic thought is the way traditional people think today and the way
others thought in the past. It is a reasonable way of ordering the world that
presupposes any activity can happen again. Thus, the telling of a cosmogonic myth continues creation. It re-creates. It is unfortunate that our
Western use of the word "myth" connotes "falsehood"[3] when what is wanted
is a term to express the structure of meaning, not fiction. As noted earlier,
we are the product of almost 2,500 years of enervating desacralization.
Lacking belief in our visions, we have, instead, hermeneutics: we "interpret"
dreams. Our ancestors, as do traditional peoples today, *understood their
dreams*. They could activate them, make them happen. Nonetheless, we
persist in thinking in symbolic terms (as though we could think in any other
way, and in truth we cannot). As Mircea Eliade explains, we carry with us a
"...quantity of mythological litter   [in] ill-controlled zones of our minds."[4]
What could this "mythological litter" be? Claude Lévi-Strauss describes this
phenomenon not so much as a "quantity of mythological litter" but as "ex-
planatory cells"[5] whose content may change but whose structure stays the
same because our nervous systems mediate between mind and experience,
patterning the data. We think, in other words, as we must. We can change
the metaphor, but not the metaphorical activity. By looking for the struc-
tural constant we can determine meaning. Lévi-Strauss calls this "...the
quest for the invariant, or for the invariant element among superficial differences."[6]   Thus, by collecting many myths, we can find common coor-
dinates, perhaps enough to see structure. Eliade, on the other hand, draws
our attention to the symbol *qua* symbol, stressing that its multivalent nature
is precisely what renders the symbol "...consubstantial with human existence,
[coming] before language and discursive reason." "...bringing to light the
most hidden modalities of being."[7]   In other words, the symbol as archetype.

Lévi-Strauss' approach has the advantage of optimism. It leads one to
believe that personal thinking is understandable, if not replicable, by
others — no matter when or where — that we are not victims of western his-
toricism. Eliade's approach has the advantage of specificity. We start first
with the image (the sunrise, the mound), the symbol *qua* symbol. If we find
enough of them, we have an archetype. Since archetypes are religious, we

are then in a position to start "...from any stylistically and historically condi-tioned creation of the spirit [to] regain the vision of the archetype."[8]

Myths tell us about archetypes. Myths are true stories, true because they are, in Eliade's words, "sacred," "exemplary," and "significant."[9] Cosmogonic myths, especially, are true "...because the existence of the World is there to prove it: the myth of the origin of death is equally true because man's mortality proves it, and so on."[10] Both Lévi-Strauss' and Eliade's approaches support a search of Amerindian myth, particularly the cosmogonic myths of the Woodlands and Plains people, for directional constructs—if putting a body into a sun-warmed mound is a sacred action, that is. This chapter, therefore, reviews a number of cosmogonic myths, specifically those of human creation from Plains and Woodlands people. The myths cited, for the most part, indicate east, the rising sun, is a beneficent, life-creating, provident direction. Human creation is emphasized because the mound is a place of interment for human bones, human bodies.[11] (N.B.: Although care has been taken in compiling the review, by no means is the selection derived from a comprehensive study of initial contact writings.)

Sacramental Function

We know the Amerindian myths both as stories and, less well, through the rituals they are part of. They function sacramentally today. There are rules for their telling—when they may be told, to whom, and in what circumstance. As Joseph Epes Brown explains: "Among Native American peoples, it is generally true myths may be told only after dark and normally in the winter season, after the last thunder of summer and before the first thunder of spring. It is at this time that beings of dangerous influence are absent, bears, snakes, and spiders among some peoples, for example."[12] The reason for this is that the retelling of the myth animates the story and makes it all happen again—on another sphere of existence, but not so far away that such power could not break through into our own plane of being. And that would be terrifying. Myths are true in that sense. They pulse in the telling of them. The language is vibrant in a sacred way. For the Ojibway, Irving Hallowell reports, the myth itself is a "...conscious being, with powers of thought and action."[13] We have many examples of this sort of vibrant formulary in other religions—where speaking the god's words, the shaman's words, the mystic's words in a worthy way makes the deed happen again, the metamorphoses occur. Åke Hultkrantz's description of the Amerindian myth is worth quoting in full as it helps us recognize the myth, and separate it from legendary or folklore aspects: "It [the myth] takes place at the beginning of time, its acting personages are gods and mythic beings like the culture hero, primeval man, and the prototypes of animals, and the scene for action is the supernatural world. The myth has a fixed pattern of events, and actions are often repeated four times in North American texts."[14]

The Rising Sun in Woodlands and Plains Myth

In 1984, Richard Erdoes and Alfonso Ortiz published their collection of 166 well-known Amerindian myths under the title *American Indian Myths and Legends* (New York: Pantheon Books, 1984). The stories were collected over the last twenty-five years from Amerindian elders they interviewed, or are accounts collected in the nineteenth century and regarded as authentic ethnographic data. Although Erdoes and Ortiz made no differentiation between "legend" and "myth," most folklorists do. Erdoes and Ortiz use "legend" and "myth" as interchangeable terms, saying of the stories: "They are emblems of a living religion, giving concrete form to a set of beliefs and traditions that link people living today to ancestors from centuries and millennia past."[15] Many of the stories collected are from Woodlands and Plains peoples. The stories display frequently a concern with directionality and with the sun. For example, in the section devoted to tales of human creation, the White River Sioux tell of Rabbit Boy who made the first human being from a blood clot and then went off to wrestle with the sun.[16] The Penobscot tell of the first man, a boy, made from the foam of the waves, "...quickened by the wind and warmed by the sun,"[17] but above all the sun's warmth "...because warmth is life." At the same time, the first woman, a girl, was made of "the wonderful earth plant, and of the dew, and of warmth [the sun]. The two marry and she becomes First Mother. He is only called her "husband." They have children who starve. She instructs him to kill her, and he does at *high noon*. Following her instructions, he strips the flesh from her bones, scatters it over the fields, and buries her bones in the middle of a clearing. Seven moons later, her husband and children return to find corn growing in the fields, and tobacco where her bones had been buried.[18] (Almost always, the Adena, Hopewell, and Mississippian interments were accompanied with tobacco pipes.)

In the Brule Sioux story of "Stone Boy,"[19] the procedure for a bundle burial is described. The hero does not know how to bring the desiccated bodies of his uncles back to life. He is told what to do by *rock*: Water and warmth will revive them; construct a sweat lodge. It works. In this story fire substitutes for the sun as a life-giving power. Rocks, water, and fire are described as "purifying": "All this has been given to us so that we may live. We shall be a tribe." (One is reminded of the necessary proximity of water to the burial mound, the use of fire in cremation — and possibly by the paleo-Indian as a holy object — the purifying rite for putrefied leavenings of flesh, and of change in social organization from scattered, wandering hunting bands to tribe.)

The Seneca tale of "The Powerful Boy"[20] tells us of a Heraklean figure whose mother dies birthing him and is cremated. His father warns him never to go north, west, south, because of specific evils there. He does, of course, and, of course, overcomes all of the trials. Warned then never to go east "...where they play ball" (is this a reference to the ritual Mississippian game of chunkey?), he goes and finds a paradisiacal land. He returns for his brothers and father and moves them all to the "...great level country of beautiful plains." (One cannot help but be reminded of how E. G. Squier, too, was struck by the beautifully cleared plains about the mounds. Something there is that loves a lawn, apparently.)

In the Cheyenne tale, "The Old Woman of the Spring,"[21] the direction north is a harbinger of misfortune. Because the Cheyenne planted corn which came from the north, it was stolen from them, and: "It was a long time before the Cheyenne planted any more corn." (The Cheyenne, like other Plains people, resisted removal to reservations and conversion to Christianity and agriculture, twinned objectives in the minds of many missionaries and civil administrators.)

In the Cheyenne tale of "The Arrow Boy,"[22] a young boy whose mother had been pregnant with him for four years, is mutilated by the tribe. He leaves them after appearing to them four times in the east. A great famine ensues. He returns to them, coming from the east, and gives them the Medicine Arrows. (These arrows are today still in the safekeeping of the Arrow Keeper of the South Cheyenne.)[23] The beneficent figure who comes from the east also appears in an Ojibway tale telling of the "Legend of St. Mary's Falls," collected by John Morgan:[24] Threatened by plague, the people hope to appease the angry spirits by sacrificing a maiden at daybreak. She is to be sent over the falls in a canoe. At the critical moment a spirit maiden appears out of the east and takes her place in the canoe.

A contradictory directional element appears in the Brule Sioux version of the "White Buffalo Woman."[25] She teaches two warriors, who sought game in the early morning, how to pray, how to make an altar, how to "be human." She teaches them the sunwise direction for praying and how to hold the pipe. Then she leaves them: "The people saw her walking off in the same direction from which she had come, outlined against the red ball of the setting sun." This tale was collected in 1967, and there well may be syncretic elements in it, both religious and Hollywood. In order to pray sunwise, the only way to begin the prayer is to the east; that should have been the direction of the origin and return of White Buffalo Woman.

The Cheyenne story explaining the origin of "The Great Medicine Dance"[26] relates that this most sacred ceremony came about because a medicine man and the "most beautiful woman" received a vision while they slept on beds of sage, facing the rising sun. The vision told them to enter a mountain and learn how to perform the ceremonies of renewal, of rebirth, of fertility. They did. Then leaving the mountain's interior they returned to the village with all they had learned: "And at some time during their journey back to their village, the man and the woman did lovingly what was necessary to ensure renewal and continuation of life through womanpower." Their prayers are offered to the sun each morning. (The vivid image of the mountain calls to mind those burial mounds holding inside a centered, formal interment of a young man and a young woman along the Scioto Valley.)

The Blackfoot tale of "The Orphan Boy and the Elk Dog"[27] tells of a boy who travels four days south and brings home a horse to his tribe in the north. This story may reflect the historical wanderings of the Blackfoot and their obtaining of the horse from the descendants of ones left behind by the Spaniards.

Similarly, D. F. Pocock's studies of the Book of Genesis demonstrate a direct correlation between the "...symbolic geography of the Hebrews"[28] in Genesis and the actual travels of the Jewish people in prehistory. Pocock describes this symbolic geography as "...a kind of moral geodesy,"[29] placing north-south movement with the healing, good marriage, the spiritual qualities in the north and sterile materialism in the south. Pocock's illustration of Genesis' north-south moral geodesy is Eden and Mount Ararat to the north (northeast) and Egypt to the south (southwest), thus making east equivalent to north and south equivalent to west. The actual movement is east-west, or even possibly "sunwise." This may be an illustration, too, of how difficult it is for us who are taught to regard north as primary, as the direction at the top of the page, to think in a "sunwise" way even when provided with reason to do so.

Another Blackfoot tale, "The Sacred Weed,"[30] balances nicely the role of men and women in making tobacco grow. Both dance upon a mound they have planted with seeds stored in a medicine bundle made of the skin of a water creature because: "Sun and water mean life. Sun begets life and water makes it grow..." when all is returned to the earth, to the mound.

A Brule Sioux tale "How Grandfather Peyote came to the Indian People"[31] specifies a vision quest undertaken by an old woman and her granddaughter who huddle together without water or food until they felt "...the wingbeats of a huge bird, an eagle flying from the east toward the west." (Again, we seem to have here deliverance from need obtained from a creature who flies sunwise.)

The rest of the Ortiz-Erdoes collection, organized thematically into such sections as "tales of world creation," "tales of the sun, moon, and stars," "ordeals of the hero," reflects the same concern with directionality, especially with east the beneficent, renewing direction.

Iroquois Creation Myth

The Cayuga version of the Iroquois creation myth as compiled by John Witthoft (1966)[32] is replete with directional motifs, all involving the sun. The woman who fell from the sky-world and makes the earth does so by walking sunwise around the clod of earth on the turtle's back, which the muskrat had retrieved at her request from the murky depths. (In another version, it is a frog who is the earth diver.)[33] The earth keeps growing as she walks around it this way and later as she and her daughter walk around it.

The making of man later on in the Iroquois myth is described as something that has to be made of clay and baked in a fire.[34] (Although the earliest Amerindian clay pots were honoured grave offerings, the reference here might be a syncretic Christian element taken from the tale of Genesis where Adam is made of dust, or clay.) More interestingly, the Iroquois myth does not give us a female figure, Eve, as the source of wrong-doing in the world; but, instead, a left-handed, meat-eating twin who lives now in "...the fearful realm of the night" *in the west*; the good, vegetable-eating, right-handed twin lives in the sky-world in the daylight realm.[35] For some Iroquois, this good twin was the sun personified, Jouseka (as noted by

Pierre de Charlevoix in 1761);[36] for the Chippewa or Ojibway, the good twin personified was Manabozho, the chief wind, the "strong east wind." This latter version was collected by Paul Radin and published in 1926. It is a most interesting variant of the basic Iroquois myth. In it the twins become the four winds. An old woman is told in a dream that the girl she will birth "...should never at any time face the place of the going down of the sun."[37] Despite all precautions taken by mother and daughter, the daughter inadvertently finds herself facing west, she is instantly impregnated, and when she comes to term, in the birthing she is torn to bits, flung over all of creation, because she gave birth to the four winds, of which Manabozho is the chief. In the Wyandot version of the myth, collected in 1874, the Christian syncretic element is spelled out by the Huron elder telling the tale: After Good Brother (Jouseka) bests Evil Brother in a duel, Evil Brother announces he is going to the far west and that "...hereafter all men will go to the west after death, and so until the Christian missionaries came to our land, the spirits of dead Indians went to the west and lived there."[38] This version of the myth no doubt reflects the very real dislocation of the Woodlands Indians following European contact.

The Sunwise Turning

Among Amerindian myths, the celestial referents proliferate. The sunwise circle includes the turning of everything in the sky, day or night. For example, the Pleiades are another sunwise-moving celestial figure. They are first seen in the east in the fall; when they disappear in the spring, they are in the western sky, a movement which has been observed by Amerindian peoples across the continent for millennia. The significance of the movement for planting tribes, as reflected in their myths, is that the disappearance of the constellation signals the start of the spring planting season, the time of corn. The Pleiades in Iroquois and Cherokee myths are thought to be hungry children (as children would have been hungry in the winter if there were more mouths to feed than supplies available).[39] The Blackfoot describe these children as "...seven poor boys who, having known nothing but hunger and cold in this world, were changed into stars."[40]

Mircea Eliade reminds us that for "...archaic man, reality is a function of the imitation of a celestial archetype."[41] The sunwise turning was the natural order of things. Myth, in fact, no matter what its formulation, or its variant, always has archaic content that is constant, ordered naturally. In all of the Iroquoian genesis variants, does it matter what aquatic creature is the earth diver? What matters is a creature who bridges both earth and water. The variants point to specific manifestations still working. The variants teach respect for all manner of life. (Myths are teaching devices, too.) Does it matter if the destruction of the mother provides us with twins or with four winds? What matters is the destruction of the woman. In some versions this produces agricultural fertility—beans, squash, pumpkin, corn.

Time and again, the myths tell us that east is the beneficent, strong, sun-warming direction, and that there is, indeed, a concern with directionality. Without doubt, directionality matters, matters critically. One suspects that at no time of the day was the ancient Amerindian unaware of where the sun was in the sky, and what that placement meant. Note, for example, that one can search for days through collections of Amerindian myth and never find a concern similarly expressed for colour. Directional movements serve to move the story along, to animate the myth, to restore order, to continue the work of creation.

But where do the dead go? Is a sun-warmed earthen burial mound the final resting place, or is interment a means somehow of transformation? Of travel to some other place?

Endnotes Chapter IV

[1.] For example, the consistent use of a sunwise turning was used by all dance competition participants at the 11th Annual Odawa Pow-Wow, May 30, 1987, Nepean, Ontario. Whether it was traditional dancing or "fancy dancing," the participants turned sunwise, both as individuals and *en masse*, moving about the circle. Elders leading the opening and closing exercises entered the circle at the eastern point where a pavilion had been erected, and turned sunwise about the circle, exiting at the east.

[2.] John E. Pfeiffer, *The Creative Explosion: An Inquiry into the Origins of Art and Religion* (New York: Harper & Row, 1982), p. 185. Pfeiffer means "non-print literate." Mnenomic devices have been in use since paleolithic times. It is we who are unable to read them and hence "illiterate" in those systems.

[3.] William Safire, "On Language," *The New York Times Sunday Magazine*, May 17, 1987, p. 12.

[4.] Mircea Eliade, *Images and Symbols: Studies in Religious Symbolism* (New York: Sheed & Ward, 1961), p. 18.

[5.] Claude Lévi-Strauss, *Myth and Meaning: Five talks for radio by Claude Lévi-Strauss* (Toronto: University of Toronto Press, 1978), p. 39.

[6.] *Ibid.*, p. 8.

[7.] Eliade, *op.cit.*, p. 12.

[8.] *Ibid.*, p. 174.

[9.] Mircea Eliade, *Myth and Reality* (New York: Harper & Row, 1963), p. 1.

[10.] Eliade, *Myth and Reality*, p. 6.

[11.] The mound also functions as a "cosmic mountain" with its *mundus* surrounding; however, that archetype is not explored in this study.

[12.] Joseph Epes Brown, "The Immediacy of Mythological Message: Native American Traditions," *Native Religious Traditions*, edited by Earle H. Waugh and K. Dad Prithipaul (Waterloo: Canadian Corporation for Studies in Religion, 1977), p. 114.

[13.] A. Irving Hallowell, "Ojibwa Ontology, Behavior, and World View,"

Contributions to Anthropology: Selected papers of A. Irving Hallowell (Chicago: University of Chicago Press, 1976), p. 365.

14. Åke Hultkrantz, *Belief and Worship in Native North America* (Syracuse: Syracuse University Press, 1981), p. 10.

15. Richard Erdoes and Alfonso Ortiz, *American Indian Myths and Legends* (New York: Pantheon Books,1984), p. xv.

16. Erdoes and Ortiz, *op.cit.,* "The Rabbit Boy," pp. 5-8. White River Sioux, Jenny Leading Cloud, 1967.

17. Erdoes and Ortiz, *op.cit.,* "The Corn Mother," pp. 11-15. Penobscot, Joseph Nicolar, *et al.,* 1893.

18. In an Iroquois version of this myth collected by John Morgan in *When Morning Stars Sang Together* (Agincourt: Book Society of Canada, 1974), pp. 14-19, Gosadaya [Glooscap] prays for a more stable food source for his people. The Great Spirit gives his wife corn seed, but she is mocked by Gosadaya's brother and she leaves. As she departs, she tells her husband that in order to find her, "...you must take a long journey towards the rising sun until you come to a big waterhole." Other instructions follow. A cold wind blows from the north, people starve, Glooscap sets out to find his wife, and does. She stays with him throughout the winter, but when spring comes, she will not return to his village because her people are crying for her return. She is the corn goddess. Her people are underground. He returns with her seed for his people.

19. Erdoes and Ortiz, *op.cit.,* "Stone Boy," pp. 15-19. Brule Sioux, Henry Crow Dog, 1910.

20. Erdoes and Ortiz, *op.cit.* "The Powerful Boy," pp. 20-24. Seneca, Jeremiah Curtin and J. N. B. Hewitt, c.1910.

21. Erdoes and Ortiz, *op.cit.,* "The Old Woman of the Spring," pp. 26-28. Cheyenne, George Dorsey, 1905.

22. Erdoes and Ortiz, *op.cit.,* "The Arrow Boy," pp. 29-33. George Dorsey, 1905.

23. *Ibid.,* p. 33.

24. John Morgan, *op.cit.,* pp. 119-120.

25. Erdoes and Ortiz, *op.cit.,* "White Buffalo Woman," pp. 47-52. Brule Sioux, Lame Deer, 1967.

[26.] Erdoes and Ortiz, *op.cit.,* "The Great Medicine Dance," pp. 33-36. Cheyenne, Josie Limpy and Mrs. Medicine Bull,1972.

[27.] Erdoes and Ortiz, *op.cit.,* "The Orphan Boy and the Elk Dog," pp. 53-60. Blackfoot, George Bird Grinnell, c. 1910.

[28.] D. F. Pocock, "North and South in the Book of Genesis," *Studies in Social Anthropology: Essays in memory of E. E. Evans-Pritchard by his former Oxford colleagues,* edited by J. H. M. Beattie and R. G. Lienhardt (Oxford: Clarendon Press, 1975), p. 275.

[29.] *Ibid.,* p. 275.

[30.] Erdoes and Ortiz, *op.cit.,* "The Sacred Weed," pp. 62-65. Blackfoot, anon, nineteenth century.

[31.] Erdoes and Ortiz, *op.cit.,* "How Grandfather Peyote came to the Indian People," pp. 65-69. Brule Sioux, Leonard Crow Dog, 1970.

[32.] James Axtell, *Indian Peoples of Eastern America: A documentary history of the sexes* (New York: Oxford University, 1981), pp. 174-179.

[33.] Morgan, *op.cit.,* p. 8. Huron, n.d.

[34.] Axtell, *op.cit.,* p. 177.

[35.] *Ibid.,* p. 178.

[36.] *Ibid.,* p. 183.

[37.] Tristram P. Coffin, *Indian Tales of North America: An anthology for the adult reader* (Philadelphia: American Folklore Society, 1961), p. 27. Ojibwa/Chippewa, Paul Radin and A. B. Reagan, 1926.

[38.] Ella Elizabeth Clark, *Indian Legends of Canada* (Toronto: McClelland and Stewart, Ltd., 1960), p. 3. Wyandot / Huron, 1874.

[39.] Lynn Ceci, "Watchers of the Pleiades: Ethnoastronomy among native cultivators in northeastern North America," *Ethnohistory,* vol. XXV, p. 312. J. Mooney, 1900.

[40.] John Morgan, *op.cit.,* p. xv. Blackfoot, n.d.

[41.] Mircea Eliade, *Cosmos and History: The myth of the sacred return* (New York: Harper & Row, 1959), p. 5.

Chapter V

THE LAND OF THE DEAD

This chapter reviews late pre-contact and early historic burial practice of the Woodlands and Plains peoples for directionality factors. The questions worth asking include: Is there any particular alignment of the bodies? If so, which way? Where are the heads pointed? Why? Where do people go when they die? What direction is that place?

All of the burial data considered is from Amerindian groups who put their dead into the earth, either as a primary or as a secondary (after cremation) interment. None of the people were mound builders of any monumental scale at the time of European contact. All at one time or another have been thought to be the descendants of the ancient mound-building cultures. Surely then, we should be able to recognize in some of their burial practices customs and motifs associated with the mound-building cultures even if no consensus exists as to who of the Woodlands and Plains people is more likely or less likely to have been the ancient mound builders.

Nevertheless, these questions are worth asking because burial practice is perhaps the one religious practice least subject to innovation. The eastern directionality we have noted in the ancient myths of the Woodlands and Plains people is the same contemporary concern we find for the proper sunwise direction observed today, both in what survives of ancient religious practice and in syncretic religious Amerindian practices. East equivalent to the rising sun is demonstrated in the ancient creation of the mound builders' sacred landscapes. It ought to be evident in some way in late pre-contact or early (i.e., pre-Christian) contact burial practice. As Edward Sapir reminds us, the "...more frequent and stereotypical such a reference, the more reason, generally speaking, we have to assign the cultural element great age."[1]

We find a concern with the sunwise direction throughout all of North America in diverse Amerindian cultures, thus supporting another Sapir criterion of antiquity: The extent of territory covered tells us how old a characteristic is—wider means older. Further, according to Sapir, traits are more readily transmitted when they are "...not hedged about with secrecy or taboo"[2] because they are dispersed along trade routes.

We have all of those conditions present to make an argument that there is a sacred directionality operative in the ancient Amerindian earthwork we have been discussing. They are burial sites, the direction pre-eminent is east, and east equivalent to the rising sun is sacred. However, the argument is inconclusive, illustrative, and provocative of discussion, rather than of demonstration because the pre-contact data collected by other scholars is simply too thin for the framework.

Examples of Sacred Directionality

It is much easier to make an argument for sacred directionality in the historic period because the data is solid. Whether it is from early or late contact period, examples of verifiably sacred, eastern directionality proliferate. To name just a few among the Woodlands and Plains people not already mentioned earlier: Nanabush, the culture hero of the Algonkian, is also known as the East Wind.[3] Among the Mohawk, repentance with prayer is offered in the early morning hours, outdoors, alone, with a small fire because one is alone with the creator at sunrise.[4] The midéwiwin among the Ojibway is described as enabling one to become part of the sun and the stars.[5] The Cree "walking out ceremony" has small children circling a tree sunwise in the daylight to communicate with the spirits.[6] Moreover, the Cree hang animal bones, especially the skull, on a tree, high up, by a creek, so the morning sun will fall on it.[7] There are examples in New Mexico of very old housing facing uphill and east rather than outward and to some other direction—just to enable the morning sun to find the dwellers each day.[8] Too, the Cree hunting lodge today always has its doorway facing east, preferably facing water; but if a choice is to be made, east predominates over a water orientation.[9] Nicolas Perrot's eighteenth-century memoir on his travels about upper and lower Canada describes many everyday examples of directionality including the piercing of an infant's nose and ears as an offering to the rising sun to take pity on the baby and preserve its life.[10]

The Midéwiwin Journey

The Ojibway tale of bear's journey to bring the midéwiwin is an especially wonderful account of pre-eminent directionality. Bear emerges from layers within the earth, travels east to the sunlight, then to the ocean for the manito-migis shell, and then to the Ojibway.[11] Like the sun dance, all of the midéwiwin's complicated ritual is oriented sunwise.

When bear emerges from the center of the earth, he is white as snow (equivalent to the north wind), then yellow as a growing thing (equivalent to the west wind), then red as a growing thing (equivalent to the south wind), then black as a dead thing (equivalent to the east wind). Note that bear's journey is the reverse of sunwise. He travels north-west-south, then east. Moreover, when he arrives at east, surely the beginning of life, he is now black "...as dead things."[12] Why? Perhaps it is because bear is from the spirit world. All things are the opposite there. The ghost midéwiwin, for example, is oriented north-south, not east-west. Part of the midéwiwin ceremony requires the sacrifice of a white puppy in lieu of bear.[13] Why white? Perhaps because in death the white puppy turns black (as do all living things when dead). In that case then, the circle of life begins anew — white (puppy alive) to black (puppy dead) to red to yellow (growing things) to white. This time in the midéwiwin itself bear's journey on earth (as started by the surrogate, a sacrificed white puppy) will be sunwise, earthly, east to south to west to north. All is restored to harmony, to balance once more.

Available Burial Data

The major difficulty in making an argument for ritual directionality in the pre-contact period lies with the studies available. The only proper area of inquiry we have is burial rite because those are the "remains" in more ways than one. What has been written about the data is fascinating, but not well ordered or annotated.

Part of the difficulty lies in the specificity of the data. Burial remains are specific to individual persons. How someone is interred reflects what was done regarding one death only. We know, for example, different procedures obtained for violent or shameful deaths. A Chippewa legend describing what is necessary for the four-day journey to the land of the dead also explains that the ghost relating this information is a Chippewa chief who died in battle against the Sioux, and: "According to the old custom, he was placed in a sitting position, his back against a tree, his face towards his fleeing enemies."[14] Myths, on the other hand, are pan-tribal in many respects. That is why there are only a few sorts of genesis myths worldwide.

Another difficulty is that Amerindian remains have been badly treated by amateur archaeologists (some might call them "grave robbers"). Bones have been scattered. Dynamite has been used to open mounds. More conscientious excavators gave little attention in writing their field reports to body placement of the remains. When a geographical direction is stated — e.g., west — we often do not know if that means head to the west or feet to the west. The same difficulty obtains in material compiled by researchers into Old and New World paleolithic and archaic cultures. Very often the position of burial is described — e.g., flexed, right or left side — but not which way the head faces.[15] Nevertheless, with those cautions in mind, this chapter considers the studies of H. C. Yarrow (1880, 1881) and David Bushnell (1920) for directional features in pre-contact and historic burial data. Bushnell and Yarrow are more than usually competent studies and attempt a comprehensive survey of the data.

H. C. Yarrow's Study (1880, 1881)

H. C. Yarrow in his landmark 1880 study of Amerindian mortuary customs for the United States Bureau of Ethnology opened his report with a neat summary about why one should be concerned with mortuary customs: They provide records of early beliefs in the nature of human existence; they illustrate the relationship of the living to the dead; they say something about the mystery of the future; they depict a reverence for the wise and the good "...who may after death be wiser and better"; and they depict the hatred and fear of enemies "...who may after death have added powers of enmity in the hereafter."[16]

Åke Hultkrantz has noted that the relationship of the living to the dead is ambivalent, complicated, complex. The dead can seem to be, Hultkrantz thinks, the masters of game because they live in nature, or in clouds, or in rain spirits.[17] They are feared, but their power and protection are sought: "Occasionally ordinary dead can also grant powers, at least indirectly, through the influence of the sun."[18] Very often the dead, for both hunters and for planters, are a source of influence on the food supply.[19]

This must have some connection with the old need to return the dead to the earth, the sun-warmed earth, to grandmother earth.

In short, mortuary customs are worthy of our interest because "...in many ways," Yarrow writes, "...they exhibit the ethical standards by which conduct in human life is judged."[20]

No doubt E. B. Tylor would approve.

The late nineteenth century was a time when scholarship, ever optimistic and ever persuaded by the seeming applicability of Darwinian theory to every endeavor, was concerned to find the start of all things, including religion. Our origins were to be found in prehistory. In our prehistory, Edward Tylor posited, our ancestors looked upon their dead and understood the equivalence of soul to life to spirit to religion as "belief in Spiritual Beings" in Tylor's well-known definition. At the time of Yarrow's writing, Tylor's most important work was popular and in print — *Researches into the Early History of Mankind* (1865) and *Primitive Culture* (1871). Both studies went into several editions and influenced so many to follow — J. G. Frazer, Andrew Lang, R. R. Marrett, for example. No mention is given to Tylor in Yarrow's bibliography, but he, like Hultkrantz, seems to have been influenced by Tylor's prescient interest in the religious practice of pre-literate peoples.

In his study of Amerindian customs, Yarrow picked up a number of interesting and telling observations. He notes that "...the Indians do not talk with freedom about their dead...they fear that knowledge which may be communicated may be used to the injury of those whom they have loved, or of themselves."[21] He notes that for all the literature regarding self-mutilation as a necessary mourning rite," ...among those tribes maimed persons are rarely found."[22] A good point. Yarrow reports this practice only for the Blackfoot,[23] and the Crow.[24] Yarrow assisted at the opening of several mounds, which appear to have been from his description Adena burial sites, and states that stone cist graves were "...almost identical in construction to "...graves of the reindeer period near Solutrie, in France," sites he also assisted with the opening of in 1873.

Yarrow notes repeatedly two basic types of Ohio and Tennessee mound inhumation orientation: bodies extended in a circle, feet inward or outward, and bodies extended on an east-west axis.[25] Similarly, the Cherokee use an east-west alignment for bodies placed under stone cairns.[26] Of the Choctaw, Yarrow notes the burials where they are placed seated, facing east, and a mound piled overhead.[27] The Mandan placed skulls in a circle of 7 m to 10 m in diameter. In the center of the circle is a mound. Upon it two buffalo skulls, one male and one female, and a 7 m tall pole. Women visit the family skulls daily, bringing food, to talk. (One cannot help but be reminded of the medicine rings and the often nearby tepee rings further west.)

One of the most important customs Yarrow reports is that of the Algonkian. They provide the dead with food and a fire at the grave site for four nights to warm them because the journey to the land of the dead takes four days. The dead do not travel at night. They are tired and must rest if they are to succeed in that fearful journey. (This custom persists even today. The Ojibway mourn their dead four days when the spirit of the person is still about. They provide food for the dead by either putting it in the coffin, or by bringing it to the gravesite at night and burning it in a little fire.)[28] It would seem that the direction in which the dead go is eastward.[29] The Chippewa reported that their dead go south[30] to the shore of a great ocean. Theirs is a difficult journey and not all succeed in completing it successfully; thus, the importance of the attendant grave goods and the burial ritual mourning. (Åke Hultkrantz makes the point that grave goods are not meant to be offerings to the dead. They are placed in the grave to aid the dead by releasing their spiritual essence, or because they belonged to the dead and the survivors are fearful the dead will return for something that is dear to them.)[31]

Scaffold burials, or what Yarrow calls "aerial sepultures," are used by the Plains peoples, the Blackfoot and Dakota, for example. Other tribes using a scaffold, such as the Choctaw, do so as an interim step before cremation (exposing the flesh permits it to rot), or communal interment in a tribal feast of the dead. After the flesh is cleaned from the bones, the bones are placed in an ossuary. Yarrow reports that this practice is also followed by Florida and Carolina Indians because they think of the soul as "a bird form"[32] (which brings us to an interesting referent to the mound builders and their raptorial mortuary emblems).

Yarrow's study prompted an outpouring of shared information. People wrote to Washington confirming what he had written and adding customs of which he had not heard. The following year, the Bureau of Ethnology issued a revised edition of the study entitled *A Further Contribution to the Study of Mortuary Customs of the North American Indians* (1881). This study provided more data for a further separation of burial custom between

Plains and Woodlands peoples. For example, it was reported the Sioux bury their dead in an extended position in the direction from which they were known to have received their vision quest power,[33] unless the individual was murdered. In that case, the corpse was placed face down, head to the south, and a bit of animal fat put in the mouth.[34] (Generally, but not always, persons seeking a vision would pray to the east. That might make east the more likely direction for head placement in burial positioning.) The role of women in burial rites was elaborated upon. Seemingly, no matter where, it was women who conducted the rites, prepared the dead, and mourned them ritually. John Young, head of the Blackfoot agency in Montana, wrote to Yarrow, "...the men would not touch nor remain in proximity to a dead body."[35]

Yarrow collected carefully a good lot of information on burial customs, still one important piece of information remained unclear: where do the dead go? We are given contradictory information in response.[36] We know that no one wanted the dead to linger in the land of the living.

Åke Hultkrantz's Study (1981)

Hultkrantz dealt with this problem in his essay "The Problem of Christian Influence of Northern Algonkian Eschatology." He, too, reached no conclusion about where the land of the dead may be placed. This one people, the Algonkian, whose practices are relatively cohesive in many other cosmogonic matters, seem to have told eighteenth-century writers that the land of the dead lay to the east,[37] and to the west,[38] that it was in the sky,[39] or in the "wigwam of Grandmother Earth."[40] Similar contradictory information was elicited by later investigators although, more often than not, they were told the land of the dead was in the western sky,[41] obtained via the Milky Way,[42] a direction that might bespeak a fusion of Christian eschatology with Algonkian.

Influence of Migration

Edwin Oliver James, writing in 1928, in *American Anthropologist,* "Cremation and Preservation of the Dead," pointed out that the confusion of doctrine and practice regarding the eventual destination of the dead may be traced to an overlay of ancient memory regarding migratory journeys with later changes in religious belief: "Thus, the belief that the cremating section of a tribe went to the sky may have been succeeded by a secondary belief resulting from migration, and in this way a confusion between doctrine and practice has arisen. That something like this occurred in the New World is suggested by the abode of the dead being frequently a combination of the upper and under worlds, and a western terrestrial paradise connected with the sun and the horizon.[43] James' point of how confusion may occur is worth underlining.

Certain burial customs associated with the destination of the dead may have other referents — historic referents — long ago forgotten, particularly forgotten migrations. We know that the interconnection of the living with the dead involves a tendency to regard the original home of the people as "...the land of the dead whither ghosts returned at death."[44] This would certainly affect such aspects of funerary ritual as whether cremation or earth interment were to be chosen, and how bodies would be aligned, and what grave goods (or persons) would accompany the dead on their journey. If once the living had believed the dead returned to a real place, the ancestral home of the tribe (west or east), the belief could over time lose its specific referent and become a distant land (west or east), perhaps beyond the sea, perhaps a mythical region, an island of the blest. James refers to a sky destination as "primary" and the migratory origins as "secondary." I think it more likely the sky destination is a secondary belief. So far as we know, cremation never replaced earth interment (even cremated bones became secondary earth interments) as a preferred practice. And, of course, although James refers only to a "western celestial paradise," the point is to find out if paradise is west or east, and why, and whether it is celestial or something else.

Migratory movement will certainly account for much of the east-west variance in orientation of the burial site. That is the migratory pattern of the Amerindian since the earliest days of the paleo-Indian who followed the great rivers down, along, and across the Great Divide, then across the continent and back again. Nonetheless, the migratory patterns do not tell us why cremation and interment were practiced contemporaneously east of the Mississippi. The distinction of status and the practicality of convenience probably influenced if not dictated the varying forms, just as in our own time burial practices differ, sometimes varying even within families adhering to the same religious traditions because everything after all depends upon what the survivors are willing and able to do. Still, as noted before, be it inhumation or cremation, with both there was a return to sun-warmed earth of ashes, of bone, and of flesh in the same burial mound together.

Not so the scaffold burials. Those rituals as practiced by the Plains and Prairie peoples were fully skyward directed. The remains of the dead were not later cremated. Raptorial birds carried flesh skyward, the spirit of the dead following over the Milky Way to the west. Some said the dead were following the great grey bear as he returned home, shaking the snow off his back (the Milky Way) over the bridge of dead souls to the eternal hunting grounds.[45]

David Bushnell's Study (1920)

David Bushnell, Jr. in his text *Native Cemeteries and Forms of Burial East of the Mississippi* (1920) organized the Amerindian burial data by tribal configuration where known: Algonkian, Iroquois, Muskhogean, Sioux. A rough tally of the types of burial by tribe is thus possible. The pre-contact sites are organized by type of burial: stone-lined graves (cists), mound burial, and cave. This information taken together produces some interesting, albeit confusing, comparative configurations. The Algonkian and Muskhogean groups appear to favour mostly a burial site with an east-facing direction—whether the corpse is interred in a flexed, extended, or flexed and seated position. In other words, the corpse can see the rising sun. Only the Ojibway and the Menomini do not. Both of these peoples believe the land of the dead is westward. The Ojibway, consequently, face the body westward, generally in a seated position, in a grave so it will head off in the correct direction.[46] The Menomini do the same or use a scaffold burial before removal to a common ossuary.[47] All of the Muskhogean group (as described by Bushnell) favour an easterly orientation for the burial.

The Sioux and the Iroquois groups mostly favour a westward orientation in their burial sites because that is where the dead go, towards the setting sun.[48] Only the Cherokee do not. This presents us with an interesting problem: Of the very large Algonkian group, all hunters and all of patrilineal descent, all but two groups use an easterly (rising sun) burial orientation for the corpse. Of the very large Iroquois group, all agricultural and all of matrilineal descent, all but one group uses a westerly (setting sun) burial orientation. (The data for the Muskhogean and Sioux group is incomplete in Bushnell's text.)

Summary

What are we to say then about where the mound builders might have believed the dead went? It is difficult to say from this review of burial data. To some extent, all of the mound builders, even the Poverty Point culture people so long ago, were agricultural. We know all of the mound builders favoured an eastern directionality in their burial mounds. The answer depends on which of the historic tribes one believes to be the descendant of which of the mound-building peoples.

As noted before, the candidates include for Adena / Hopewell, the Cherokee, Algonkian, and Sioux; for the Mississippian, the Creek, Chickashaw, Choctaw, and Cherokee. Bushnell's burial data, however roughly I have tabulated it, might eliminate the Sioux from consideration as descendants of the Adena / Hopewell. The case for all the rest is strengthened because of the eastern directionality in the burial mounds. Although the relationship of east to west in burial ritual and of tribal lines of descent, matrilineal and patrilineal, is beyond the scope of my study, there probably is a relevant relationship.

Endnotes Chapter V

[1.] Edward Sapir, *Time Perspective in Aboriginal American Culture: A Study in Method* (Ottawa: Canada Department of Mines, Geological Survey, 1916), p. 17.

[2.] *Ibid.*, p. 31.

[3.] Joan Vastokas and Romas K. Vastokas, *Sacred Art of the Algonkians: A Study of the Peterborough Petroglyphs* (Peterborough: Mansard, 1973), p. 71.

[4.] Earle H. Waugh and K. Dad Prithipaul, eds., *Native Religious Traditions* (Waterloo: Canadian Corporation for Studies in Religion, 1979), p. 37.

[5.] *Ibid.*, p. 38.

[6.] Adrian Tanner, *Bringing Home Animals: Religious ideology and mode of production of the Mistassini Cree hunters* (Newfoundland: Memorial University Institute of Social and Economic Research, 1979), pp. 91-92.

[7.] *Ibid.*, p. 92.

[8.] Nelson A. Reed, "Monks and other Mississippian Mounds," *Explorations into Cahokia Archaeology*, edited by Melvin L. Fowler (Urbana: University of Illinois, 1973), p. 15.

[9.] Tanner, *op.cit.*, p. 101.

[10.] James Axtell, *Indian Peoples of Eastern America: A documentary history of the sexes* (New York: Oxford University Press, 1981), p. 13.

[11.] Ruth Landis, *Ojibwa Religion and the Midéwiwin* (Madison: University of Wisconsin Press, 1968), pp. 106-108.

[12.] As recorded by Elizabeth Tooker in *Native North American Spirituality of the Eastern Woodlands* (New York: Paulist Press, 1979), p. 228, the Winnebago tobacco offering to the spirits seems to display a similar ambivalence about east. The order of the offering is first to the father who dwells above; then west to the grandfather thunderbird chief; then east, "you who walk in darkness"; then south, "disease giver," then to the sun, "grandfather who brings day"; then earth as grandmother; and lastly moon as grandmother "who comes at night." This is neither a sunwise nor reverse sunwise direction. There is no mention of north. Above is not equivalent to north, nor are mentions of celestial figures to be thought equivalent to north.

13. Landis, *op.cit.*, p. 181.

14. Ella Elizabeth Clark, *Indian Legends of Canada* (Toronto: McClelland and Stewart, Ltd., 1960), p. 68.

15. It may be that directional factors slide past Western researchers because today's Christian cemeteries lack specific directional orientation, although early Christians often insisted upon interment with feet pointed east, "toward Jerusalem," or one might say, "facing the rising sun."

16. H. C. Yarrow, *Introduction to the Study of Mortuary Customs among the North American Indians* (Washington: Bureau of Ethnology, 1880), p. 3.

17. Åke Hultkrantz, *Belief and Worship in Native North America* (Syracuse: Syracuse University Press, 1981), p. 111.

18. *Ibid.*, pp. 99-100.

19. *Ibid.*, p. 102.

20. Yarrow, *op.cit.*, p. 4.

21. *Ibid.*, p. 5.

22. *Ibid.*, p. 6.

23. *Ibid.*, p. 67.

24. *Ibid.*, p. 90.

25. *Ibid.*, pp. 20-23.

26. *Ibid.*, p. 60.

27. *Ibid.*, pp. 25-29.

28. Joe Morrison, interviewed by Peter Meggs on "Open House," CBC-FM, May 3, 1987.

29. Yarrow, *op.cit.*, p. 103.

30. *Ibid.*, pp. 104-105.

31. Hultkrantz, *op.cit.*, p. 95.

32. Yarrow, *op.cit.*, p. 75.

[33.] H. C. Yarrow, *A Further Contribution to the Study of Mortuary Customs of the North American Indians* (Washington: Bureau of Ethnology, First Annual Report, 1881), p. 107.

[34.] Yarrow, *A Further Contribution to...*, p. 107.

[35.] *Ibid.*, p. 161.

[36.] For example, Yarrow writes in *Introduction to the Study of Mortuary Customs*, p. 95, that the Huron and others reported the dead were bound for the land of the dead "...situated in the regions of the setting sun." If so, one must keep in mind Yarrow's opening caveat that the Amerindian were chary of speaking of their dead lest harm come to the dead. How many times were people asked at graveside where did the dead go? Would an informant give a deliberately misleading answer? One might not want to answer other than indirectly if harmful spirits were about looking for the dead.

[37.] Hultkrantz, *op.cit.*, p. 199.

[38.] *Ibid.*, p. 194.

[39.] *Ibid.*, p. 196.

[40.] *Ibid.*, p. 208.

[41.] *Ibid.*, p. 207.

[42.] *Ibid.*, p. 209.

[43.] E. O. James, "Cremation and the Preservation of the Dead in North America," *American Anthropologist*, vol. XXX (1928), p. 233.

[44.] *Ibid.*, p. 233.

[45.] John S. Morgan, *When Morning Stars Sang Together* (Agincourt: Book Society of Canada, 1974), p. xv.

[46.] David I. Bushnell, Jr., *Native Cemeteries and Forms of Burial East of the Mississippi* (Washington: Bureau of American Ethnology, 1920), p. 30.

[47.] *Ibid.*, p. 25.

[48.] *Ibid.*, p. 77.

Chapter VI

FINAL CONSIDERATIONS

Grandmother Earth

The forms devised by the mound builders to inter the bones and ashes and bodies of their dead seem to suggest the sort of referent identified elsewhere in the world as feminine in other neolithic systems. For example, the beehive tombs of Mycenae have been likened to the womb and breast of the goddess or Great Mother. There is nothing so readily demonstrable in pre-contact Amerindian structures, no matter how similar the forms, to lead us to such a neat iconographical exegesis: The matrilineal, agricultural Iroquois did not bury their dead in easterly, sun-warmed mounds of earth. If they had, we might be able to extrapolate something from that practice to an earth-formed, feminine breast or belly. We cannot. We lack an Amerindian equivalent to the womb-shaped passage graves of neolithic Europe containing hundreds of female interments, marked with the symbols of the goddess. We have nothing so specific that we can recognize in North America. What we do have, however, is an especially coherent, sophisticated, but subtle, statement of rebirth and renewal as exhibited in a sun-warmed, easterly oriented, mound interment. The mound interments appear to be expressions of faith in a necessary renewal of life, of a continuing cycle of life, that *specifically involves individual human beings in its perpetuation, a cycle of life not devoid of this world, one involving the very earth itself.* In later years, the descendants of the mound builders would come to speak of the cycle of rebirth and renewal as a connectedness with, a reverence for "Grandmother Earth," the source of life. Otherwise, why go to all that bother of constructing burial mounds of such size and complexity? Why scrape flesh from bone and scatter it among the fields?

But note, the Amerindian sense of "grandmother" is not the same as the Great Mother goddess of the Old World. Old World figures always show the goddess as powerfully sexual, wheather she is maiden, mother, or crone. Not so in many Amerindian cultures. "Grandmother" and "grandfather" are asexual honourifics of high reverence. Very often in tribal cultures, it is grandmother who nourishes, protects, and teaches the child. Among the Ojibway today, it is St. Anne, the *grandmother* of Christ, who is the most revered feminine figure in Catholicism, not Mary, the *virgin* mother.

Cosmological Balance

There are other forms of disposal of the dead the mound builders might have used. They might have built funeral pyres and scattered the ashes to the wind. They might have floated bodies in canoes downstream. They might have abandoned their dead to things "that go bump in the night" in the forest. They did none of these things. For many generations they retrieved the bones of their dead and brought them back to the mounds.

Any other burial practice but a mound interment would have changed the cosmological balance of earth, sun, and water which was fully realized in a mound interment of the Adena / Hopewell and Mississippian periods. And, in fact, in later years the balance did shift when mounds were no longer built, earth corridors no longer constructed to the riverbank. People moved elsewhere and attention shifted skywards. Bodies were left exposed on high platforms in some areas, not in all. The journey to the land of the dead was told as somewhere over the Milky Way. In older myths, the journey had been over a bridge, the bridge crossing a river, and the land on the other side, pleasant, warm, and fertile.

There is a reason why this latter concept is probably the older myth, and why the land of the dead was probably understood to be right at hand, not in a skyworld elsewhere, for the mound builders who symbolized their belief by building mounds in an easterly manner near water.

Most people who died were not shamans. Few ever are. As Joseph Epes Brown reminds us, only the shaman was "...able to travel at will through the freedom of sacred space unfettered by mechanical, profane time."[1] For everyone else architecture was protection from the unknown, the "things that go bump in the night." Tomb architecture then was most important. That is why it mimicked dwelling house shape, circular or later rectangular. It fixed people to the earth, indubitably returning them to *terra firma*, to grow again. Time and time again, Amerindian architecture, whether it be the sun dance lodge, the midéwiwin lodge, the big house, has always been explained as a model of the world, the world made human, the world as flesh. Thus, one may imagine that the mound builders returned their dead to the earth in order that they be made flesh (in the sense of "alive") again. That is why they were anointed with red ochre.

The Adena / Hopewell and Mississippian burial sites should be thought of as sacred landscapes. And as sacred landscapes, we may have here nascent illustrations of the historic Amerindian religious concepts of *manitou, wakan, orenda*.

These concepts are not easily understood. Too often they have been described as a "supernatural sort of potency," a spiritual power, as though the concept were something otherworldly, ladled out in dribs and drabs by the Great Spirit, the Great Manitou, the great-being-wherever in the sky. In other words, as though *manitou-wakan-orenda* were something equivalent to the Christian notion of grace obtained through good works from a beneficent god. It is not. One could think of *wakan*, or *orenda*, or *manitou* in that sense were it not for the Amerindian persistence in also saying that certain objects or phenomena, regardless of what one does, are imbued with a sacred potency, too. One has to have a certain "clearness" perhaps to be able to see it, but the potential is always there. So there we have it — a concept both trans-energetic and object-specific. (Gifted artists might be able to deal with that sort of vibratory tension, but the rest of us must avoid distorting the concept by relating it to an otherworldly metaphysic). *Manitou-wakan-orenda is of this world particularly, although admittedly rarefied.*

Linguistic Balance

The Algonquian languages, however, render this distinction absolutely ordinary. All dualism, even "spiritual" and "secular," can be subsumed into an everyday grammar anyone can use. Thus, any landscape may be sacred, if one knows the applicable vocabulary. The vocabulary will tell you whether the object is *wakan, orenda, manitou*, whether it has potency. It is explained best as a matter of gender.

In the Algonquian languages gender is distinguished as animate or inanimate — not as male, female, and neuter. All verbs and nouns are readily identifiable as to gender. Animate nouns take animate verbs only; inanimate nouns take inanimate verbs. Animate nouns include such things as persons, animals, some objects, some plants, e.g., tobacco, corn, pipe, kettle. (Leonard Bloomfield has compiled a short gender list to explain this distinction in his essay "Algonquian," *Linguistic Structures of Native America* [1946] which is considered the classic reference.) What is intriguing about the animate objects usually cited is that they are also the ones that appear from time to time in medicine bundles. They have, therefore, it would seem by their very names alone potentially the importance of becoming or being vehicles of *manitou-wakan-orenda*. What they do not have is the potential of being delimited sexually.[2] Thus, earth, the sun-warmed earth, is not necessarily "mother earth." That is probably a European transposition. It may be enough that earth be sun-warmed, life-giving, the source in combination with water and the sun of rebirth and birth. Similarly *manitou* need not be *Great Manitou, He.* It is *manitou* and that is enough.

This is just the sort of concept so difficult for another to grasp working from a European language base where "religious" has much to do with being able to separate out that which is sacred from that which is secular. Just as there is no word for "art" in the Algonquian languages, so too is there no word for "religious." As explained earlier, myths in Amerindian culture are living narrations. They have soul, not soul as a European religious term, but soul as in "soulful"—as the word would be used today in a black American ghetto—"signifyin'"—alive, percolating, and non-Western.

Allied to the importance of gender in the Algonquian languages are Cecil Brown's observations *re* the origin of cardinal directional terms in a number of Amerindian languages. Brown compiled data from 127 languages worldwide, including 15 Amerindian languages, mostly Woodlands and Plains, and discovered that directional terms do not enter language willy nilly, and certainly not in accordance to any mapmaker's convention. Directional terms have a predictable sequence. North is not the first term. Far from it. Some languages omit it all together. If the language has terms for north and south, it will have terms for east and west. But, it is much more typical that any language having terms for east and west will not have terms for north and south.[3] In other words, the first directional term almost always in any language is east, and the word for east is almost always "rising sun,"[4] then west.[5] The word for west does not always mean "setting sun," quite often it means "disappear," or "drop," and sometimes it refers to a geographical site. For example, the Osage word for west refers to a cliff.

(One may surmise that is where the sun sets.) Then, critically important for our interests is Brown's finding that the next set of directional terms added to language is up and down, not north and south.[6] (One cannot help but think of the importance worldwide of the shaman's pole, the *axis mundi*, the tree of life, the sacred mountain.) When north and south finally appear in a language, any language, in North America south means the "daylight sun," or the "moving sun," or the "turning sun." North, however, is almost always a maleficent direction. North is entirely missing from the Atapaka, Choctaw, and Shoshoni languages. (One can get along without asking for such troubles, apparently.)

Conclusion

What all of the above suggests for our problem of directionality in Amerindian burial sites is that the cultural and psychological awareness of east "equivalent to the rising sun" is very ancient, indeed. It has a pre-eminent, consistent importance displayed in so many ways that we can only call it "sacred," understanding by that, that we mean rebirth, renewal, alive, re-creation.

One may well wish to question then whether the land of the dead was ever really in the west before the European missionaries came to ask its location. It may have been, in a most sacred way, right in front of their noses, immanent in all the world surrounding as *wakan-orenda-manitou* and, once earlier, transeunt in the sunwise burial mounds of the ancient mound builders of the Mississippi River valley.

Endnotes Chapter VI

[1] Joseph Epes Brown, "The Roots of Renewal," *Seeing with a Native Eye*, edited by Walter Holden Capps (New York: Harper & Row, 1976), p. 30.

[2] A. Irving Hallowell, "Ojibwa Ontology, Behavior, and World View," *Contributions to Anthropology: Selected Papers of A. Irving Hallowell* (Chicago: University of Chicago Press, 1976), pp. 368-369.

[3] Cecil H. Brown," Where do Cardinal Directions Come From?" *Anthropological Linguistics*, summer 1983, p. 144.

[4] *Ibid.*, p. 145.

[5] *Ibid.*, p. 145.

[6] *Ibid.*, p. 146.

Chapter VII

ILLUSTRATIONS

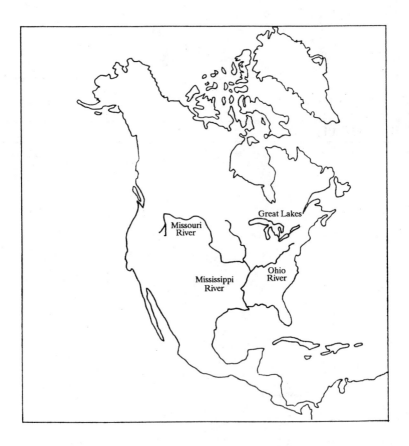

1. Amerindian migration routes. *Donna Silver*

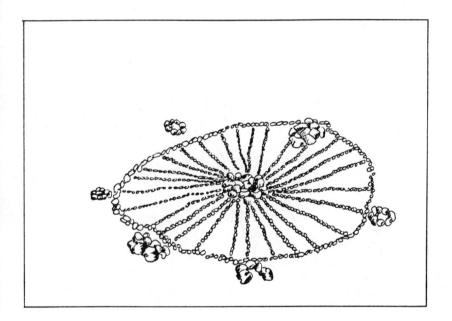

2. Aerial view of Big Horn Medicine Wheel. *Donna Silver*

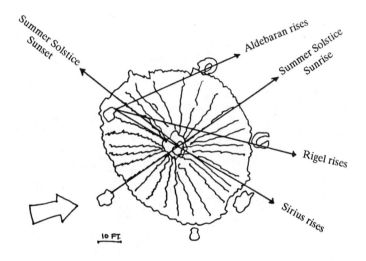

3. Cairn alignments at Big Horn Medicine Wheel. *Eddy (1975) from Native American Astronomy, edited by Anthony F. Aveni, ©1975 by University of Texas Press. Reproduced by permission of the author and the publisher.*

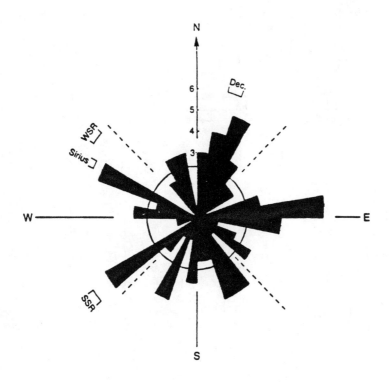

4. Distribution of (true) compass directions (azimuths) of spokes and other directional features of 20 medicine wheel sites. Circle of center is for random distribution. SSR (summer solstice sunrise); WSS (winter solstice sunrise). *Eddy (1975) from Native American Astronomy, edited by Anthony F. Aveni, ©1975 by University of Texas Press. Reproduced by permission of the author and the publisher.*

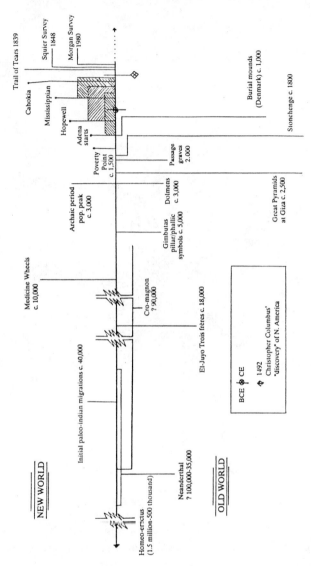

5. Selected Old and New World paleolithic and neolithic cultural milestones. *Donna Silver*

6. St. Petersburg shell mound c.1903; l. to r. Mrs. Clara Blake, Mrs. James R. Hamilton, rest unknown. *E. K. Hamilton, neg. 5683, Florida State Archives*

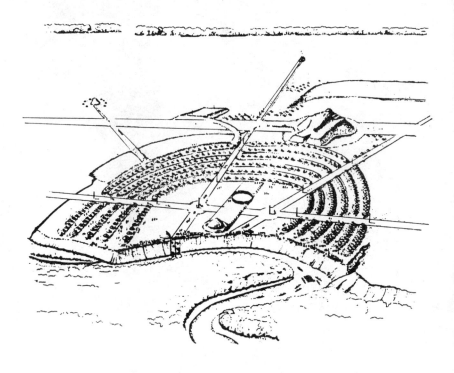

7. Reconstruction of the central district of the Poverty Point
Site about 1000 BCE. *Reprinted by permission of Jon L. Gibson*

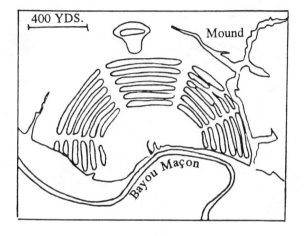

8. Poverty Point site, showing presumed effect of erosion from the bayou Maçon. *Donna Silver after Forbis (1975)*

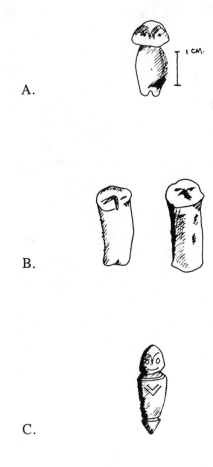

9.   a.   Poverty Point "owl" effigy bead, Louisiana c.1500 BCE, jasper. *Donna Silver after Forbis (1975)*

     b.   Pillar/phallic symbol, Romania c.5300-5000 BCE, alabaster. *Reprinted with permission of Marija Gimbutas*

     c.   Paleo-Indian talisman, Saskatchewan n.d.. *Donna Silver after Orchard (1942)*

10. Edisto Island (Fig Island), Archaic: oyster shell rings, c.76 m in outside diameter; 9-12 m high encircling wall. Dwellings may have surrounded the rings. ©*1980 by William N. Morgan*

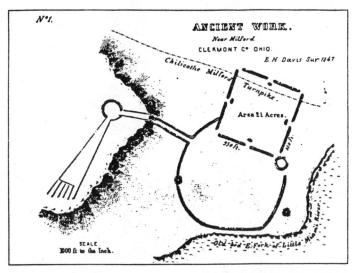

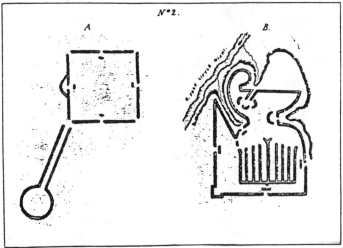

11. Ancient Work, Clermont County, Ohio, Adena. *Squier and Davis (1848)*

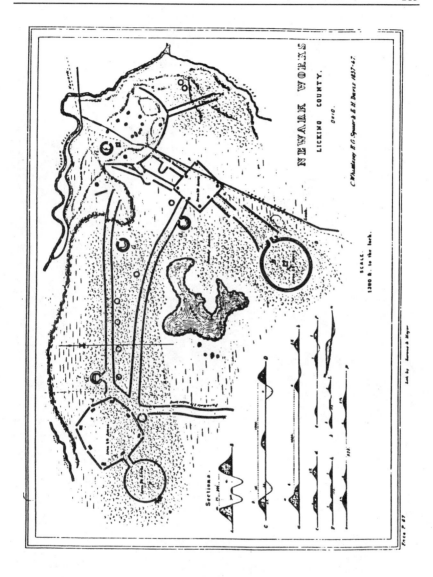

12. Newark Works, Licking County, Ohio, Adena and Hopewell combination. *Squier and Davis (1848)*

13. Burial mound, Miamisburg, Ohio, Adena. *Donna Silver*

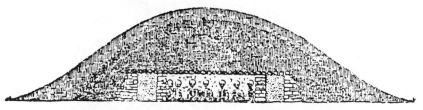

a. Mound in Jo Davies County, Illinois, section.

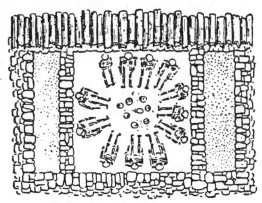

b. Mound in Jo Davies County, Illinois, base.

14.   The supposed prehistoric "Masonic burials," Jo Davies
County, Illinois, Adena.   *Reprinted by permission of the
Smithsonian Institution Press.   From "Native Cemeteries and Forms
of Burial East of the Mississippi," Bureau of American Ethnology
Bulletin no. 781, by David I. Bushnell, Jr., Smithsonian Institution,
Washington, D.C., 1920.*

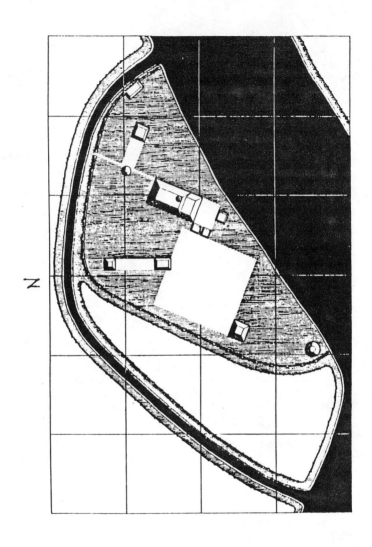

15.   Angel site, Evansville, Indiana, Mississippian.   *©1980 by William N. Morgan*

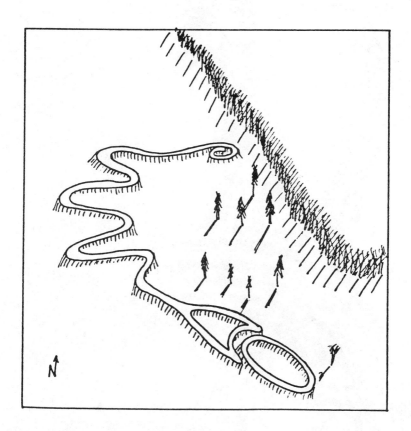

16. The Great Serpent Mound, Peebles, Ohio, Adena. *Donna Silver*

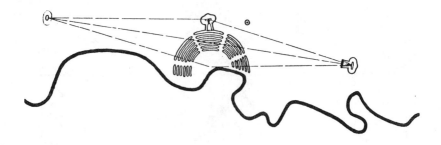

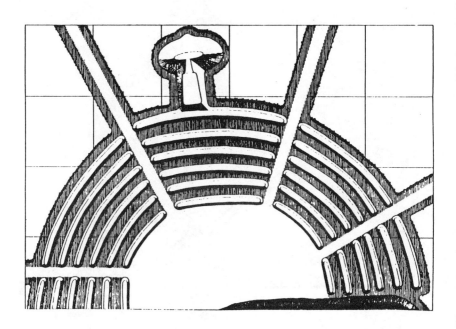

17. Poverty Point site, Louisiana, Archaic. *©1980 by William N. Morgan*

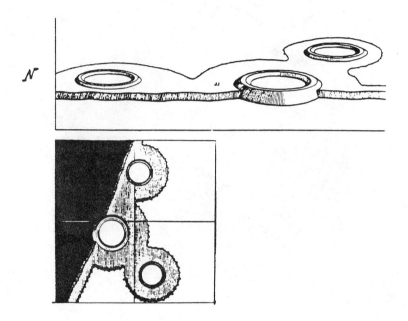

18.   Sapelo site, Sapelo Island, Georgia, Archaic.   ©*1980 by*
William N. Morgan

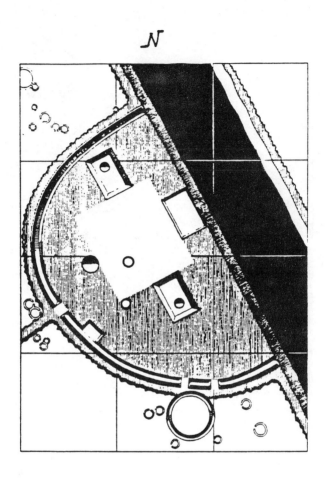

19.   Marksville, site, Marksville, Louisiana, Adena and
Hopewell. ©*1980 by William N. Morgan*

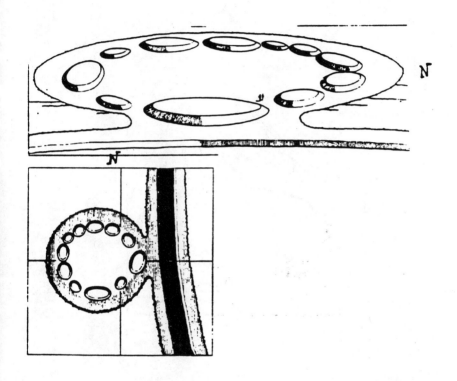

20. Tchula Lake site, Tchula, Mississippi, Adena and Hopewell.
©1980 by William N. Morgan

21. Stone Work site, Chillicothe, Ohio, Adena and Hopewell.
©*1980 by William N. Morgan*

N

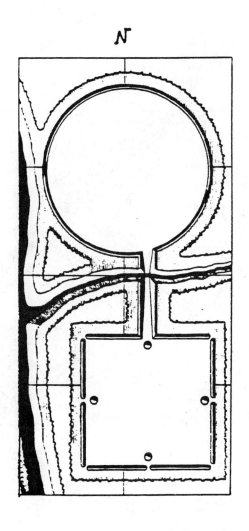

22. Seal site, Piketon, Ohio, Adena and Hopewell. *©1980 by*
William N. Morgan

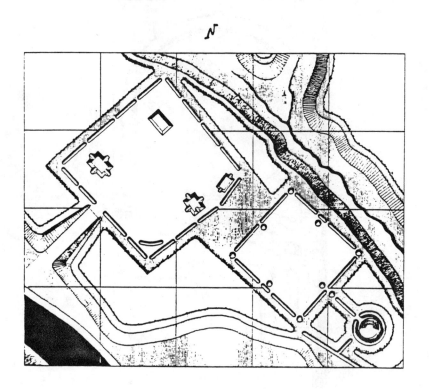

23.　Marietta site, Marietta, Ohio, Adena, Hopewell, and Mississippian. *©1980 by William N. Morgan*

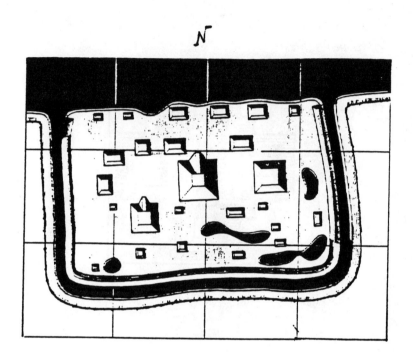

24. Lake George site, Holly Bluff, Mississippi, Mississippian.
©1980 by William N. Morgan

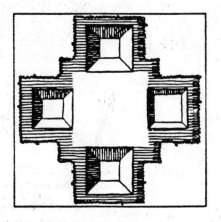

25. Alphenia site, Clayton, Louisiana, Mississippian.   ©*1980 by William N. Morgan*

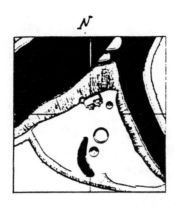

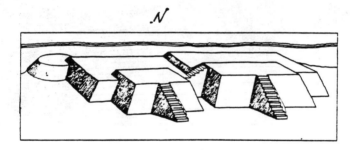

26. Hiwassee site, Dayton Tennessee, Mississippian. ©*1980 by William N. Morgan*

27. Typical dolmen construction, neolithic. *Donna Silver*

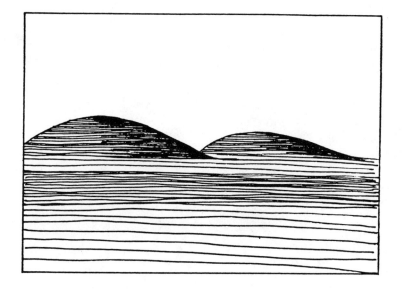

28. Burial mounds at Skøvsgård, Denmark, neolithic. *Donna Silver*

Appendix A

SUGGESTED USES FOR THE ADENA TABLET

The oblong Adena tablets have drawn a great deal of attention over the years since the first ones were discovered in the ancient burial mounds of the Adena / Hopewell period in the Ohio Valley. They are beautifully incised tablets of stone. The carvings have always seemed meaningful to investigators, as though they were a sort of hieroglyph to be translated. Many have tried. Every sort of reading was proposed in the nineteenth century, Urdu to Icelandic — all in hindsight clearly preposterous. Only about a dozen are known, similar in style, and found in the same small area of the Ohio Valley.

The design motifs are few. Arranged about a central axis, one finds raptorials, birds, carrion-eaters, birdheads, claws. Feline heads and a human hand with an eye on the palm (usually shown as though it were both a front and a back hand) are found; so, too, a smiling human face. David W. Penney describes the overall arrangement as heraldic.[1] Indeed, the orderliness and compact nature of the tablet designs do remind one of the totemic designs of the northwest coast of Canada. The tablets are small, only about 7 cm x 10 cm usually[2] and grooved on the plain reverse of the tablet.

Some have thought the tablets were printing stamps for cloth or skin.[3] David Brose declares: "Without question the traces of pigment on these tablets suggest their use as stamps, possibly for decorating organic materials, such as cloth, articles of clothing, or bark house walls."[4] Several tablets do have red and brown pigment residue in the design carving and in the worn grooves of the reverse. The pigment might have been red ochre mixed with animal fat, or even human blood.[5] If so, the tablets, indeed, represent a very sacred and very precious skilled craft practiced only in this one small area.   Unfortunately, no examples of materials known to have been printed survived.

On the other hand, Ralph Coe speculates that the tablets were used for ceremonial blood-letting.[6]   Surely they are too small for that purpose, unless he means, as others have suggested, that the tablets were used as whetstones for sharpening bone awls,[7] and these were used in blood-letting. Not necessarily, however, does one have to suppose a "ceremonial blood-letting." A whetstone would be a useful addition to anyone's tool kit for a journey to the next life.   Grave goods more often than not seem to be useful items, if especially fine ones, because one wants to present the best appearance possible on the journey.   Moreover, the living do not want the dead to return to fetch some dear item forgotten.

An alternative to the whetstone hypothesis is the posibility that the tablets are palettes for grinding pigment for textile printing.[8] This belief is held by David W. Penney. Somehow, though, grinding pigment on the back of the printing stamp itself seems a less-than-efficient way of working, no matter how ceremonial the intent.   Moreover, plain Adena tablets with worn grooves on one or both sides have also been found with pigment residue in the grooves.[9]

Why not think of the tablets as cosmetic palettes used to grind pigment for body painting? One of the interred Adena graves contained a carefully painted skull, possibly female, decorated with two bars across the forehead, crossed by one bar extending from forehead to mouth.[10]

Endnotes Appendix A

[1.] David W. Penney, "The Adena Engraved Tablets: A study of prehistory," *Native North American Art History: Selected readings*, edited by Zena Pearlstone Mathews and Aldona Jonaitis (Palo Alto: Peek Publications, 1982).

[2.] For example, the Allen tablet is 5.1 cm x 8.9 cm; the Berlin tablet is 7.1 cm x 14.3 cm.

[3.] Jesse David Jennings, *Prehistory of North America* (New York: McGraw-Hill Books, 1974), p. 227.

[4.] David S. Brose, "The Woodland Period," *Ancient Art of the American Woodland Indians*, eds. David W. Brose, James W. Brown, David W. Penney (New York: Harry N. Abrams, 1985), p. 53.

[5.] Penney, *op.cit.*, p. 268.

[6.] Ralph T. Coe, *Sacred Circles: Two thousand years of North American Indian art* (London: Arts Council of Great Britain, 1976), p. 54.

[7.] Penney, *op.cit.*, p. 271.

[8.] *Ibid.*, p. 272.

[9.] *Ibid.*, p. 271.

[10.] *Ibid.*, p. 268.

SELECTED BIBLIOGRAPHY

de Angulo, Jaime. *Coyote Man and Old Doctor Loon.*, San Francisco: Turtle Island Foundation, 1973.

Aveni, Anthony F., ed. *Archaeoastronomy in Pre-Columbian America.* Austin: University of Texas, 1977.

_____. *Native American Astronomy.* Austin: University of Texas Press, 1975.

_____. "Possible Astronomical Orientations in Ancient Mesoamerica." *Archaeoastronomy in Pre-Columbian America.* Edited by Anthony F. Aveni. Austin: University of Texas Press, 1977, pp. 163-190.

Axtell, James. *Indian Peoples of Eastern America: A documentary history of the sexes.* New York: Oxford University, 1981.

Baity, Elizabeth Chesley. "Mesoamerican Archaeoastronomy So Far." *Archaeoastronomy in pre-Columbian America.* Edited by Anthony F. Aveni. Austin: University of Texas Press, 1977, pp. 379-393.

Bernal, Ignacio. "Concluding Remark." *Prehistoric Man in the New World.* Edited by Jesse D. Jennings and Edward Norbeck. Chicago: University of Chicago Press, 1963, pp. 559-566.

Bloomfield, Leonard. "Algonquian." *Linguistics Structures of Native America.* Edited by Cornelius Osgood. New York: The Viking Fund Publications in Anthropology, nr. 6, 1946, pp. 85-129.

Britt, Claude, Jr. "Early Navajo Astronomical Pictographs in Canyon de Chelly, Northeastern Arizona, USA." *Archaeoastronomy in Pre-Columbian*

America. Edited by Anthony F. Aveni. Austin: University of Texas Press, 1977, pp. 89-107.

Brose, David S. "Late Prehistory of the Upper Great Lakes Area." *Handbook of North American Indians.* Vol. 15: *Northeast.* Washington: Smithsonian Institution, 1978, pp. 560-582.

_____. "The Woodland Period." *Ancient Art of the American Woodland Indians.* eds. David S. Brose, James W. Brown, David W. Penney. New York: Harry N. Abrams, 1985, pp. 43-91.

_____. Brown, James A., and Penney, David W. *Ancient Art of the American Woodland Indians.* New York: Harry N. Abrams, 1985.

Brown, Cecil H. "Where do Cardinal Directions come from?" *Anthropological Linguistics*, summer 1983, pp. 121-161.

Brown, Ian W. *The Role of Salt in Eastern North American Prehistory.* Baton Rouge: Louisiana Archaeological Survey and Antiquities Commission, Anthropological Study nr. 3, 1981.

Brown, James A. "The Mississippian Period." *Ancient Art of the American Woodland Indians.* eds. David S. Brose, James A. Brown, David W. Penney. New York: Harry N. Abrams, 1985, pp. 92-145.

_____. "Spiro Art and its Mortuary Contexts." *Native North American Art History: Selected readings.* Edited by Zena Pearlstone Mathews and Aldona Jonaitis. Palo Alto: Peek Publications, 1982, pp. 459-481.

Brown, Joseph Epes. "The Immediacy of Mythological Message: Native American Traditions." *Native Religious Traditions.* Edited by Earle H. Waugh and K. Dad Prithipaul. Waterloo: Canadian Corporation for Studies in Religion, 1977, pp. 101-116.

_____. "The Roots of Renewal." *Seeing with a Native Eye.* Edited by Walter Holden Capps. New York: Harper & Row, 1976. pp. 25-34.

Bushnell, Jr., David I. *Native Cemeteries and Forms of Burial East of the Mississippi.* Washington: Bureau of American Ethnology, Bulletin 71, 1920.

Campbell, Joseph. T*he Masks of Gods: Primitive mythology.* New York: Penquin Books, 1969.

_____. *The Mythic Image.* Princeton: Princeton University Press, 1974.

Ceci, Lynn. "Watchers of the Pleiades: Ethnoastronomy among native cultivators in northeastern North America." *Ethnohistory*, Vol. XXV, pp. 301-317.

Claibourne, Robert. *The Emergence of Man: The first Americans.* New York: Time-Life Books, 1973.

Clark, Ella Elizabeth. *Indian Legends of Canada.* Toronto: McClelland and Stewart, Ltd., 1960.

Coe, Michael D. "Death and the Afterlife in pre-Columbian America: Closing remarks." *Death and the Afterlife in pre-Columbian America: A conference at Dumbarton Oaks, October 27,1973.* Edited by Elizabeth P. Benson. Washington: Harvard University Press, 1975, pp. 190-195.

Coe, Ralph T. *Sacred Circles: Two thousand years of North American Indian art.* London: Arts Council of Great Britain, 1976.

Coffin, Tristram P. *Indian Tribes of North America: An anthology for the adult reader.* Philadelphia: American Folklore Society, 1961.

Cowan, Thaddeus M. "Effigy Mounds and Stellar Representation: A comparison of Old World and New World alignment schemes." *Archaeoastronomy in Pre-Columbian America*, edited by Anthony F. Aveni. Austin: University of Texas Press, 1977, pp. 217-234.

Cowan, William. Personal communication, March 18, 1987. Carleton University, Ottawa: Linguistics Department.

Eddy, John A. "Medicine Wheels and Plains Indian Astronomy." *Native American Astronomy.* Edited by Anthony Aveni. Austin: University of Texas Press, 1975, pp. 147-169.

Eliade, Mircea. *Cosmos and History: The myth of the sacred return.* New York: Harper & Row, 1959, pp. 1-92.

_____. *From Primitives to Zen: A thematic sourcebook in the History of Religions.* New York: Harper & Row, 1967.

_____. *Images and Symbols: Studies in religious symbolism.* New York: Sheed & Ward, 1961.

_____. "Methodological Remarks on the Study of Religious Symbolism." *The History of Religions: Essays in Methodology.* Edited by Mircea Eliade and Joseph M. Kitagawa. Chicago: University of Chicago Press, 1959, pp. 86-107.

_____. *Myth and Reality.* New York: Harper & Row, 1963.

_____. *Myths, Dreams, and Mysteries: The encounter between contemporary faiths and archaic realities.* New York: Harper Torchbooks, 1960.

_____. *The Quest: History and meaning in religion.* Chicago: University of Chicago Press, pp. 72-111.

_____. *The Two and the One.* New York: Harper & Row, 1962, pp. 125-159.

Ellis, Florence Hawley. "A Thousand Years of the Pueblo Sun-Moon-Star Calendar." *Archaeoastronomy in Pre-Columbian America.* Edited by Anthony F. Aveni. Austin: University of Texas Press, 1975,. pp. 59-87.

Erdoes, Richard and Ortiz, Alfonso. *American Indian Myths and Legends.* New York: Pantheon Books, 1984.

Essenpreis, Patricia. Personal communication, May 29, 1987. University of Florida, Gainsville: Department of Anthropology.

Fagan, Brian. "Who were the Mound Builders?" *Mysteries of the Past.* Edited by L. Casson, and others. New York: American Heritage Publishing Co., 1977, pp. 118-135.

Farb, Peter. *Man's Rise to Civilization as shown by the Indians of North America from Primeval Times to the Coming of the Industrial State.* New York: E. P. Dutton, 1965.

Fitting, James E. "Prehistory: An Introduction." *Handbook of North American Indians.* Vol. 15: *Northeast.* Washington: Smithsonian Institution, 1978.

_____. "Regional Cultural Development: 300 BC to AD 1000." *Handbook of North American Indians.* Vol. 15: *Northeast.* Washington: Smithsonian Institution, 1978, pp. 44-57.

Forbis, Richard G. "Eastern North America." *North America.* Edited by Shirley Gorenstein. New York: St. Martin's Press, 1975, pp. 74-102.

Fowler, Melvin L. "The Cahokia Site." *Explorations into Cahokia Archaeology.* Illinois Archaeological Survey, Inc., Bulletin 7. Urbana: University of Illinois, 1973, pp. 1-30.

_____. and Hall, Robert L. "Late Prehistory of the Illinois Area." *Handbook of North American Indians.* Vol. 15: *Northeast.* Washington: Smithsonian Institution, 1978, pp. 560-568.

Funk, Robert E. "Post-Pleistocene Adaptations." *Handbook of North American Indians.* Vol. 15: *Northeast.* Smithsonian Institution, 1978, pp. 16-27.

Gibson, Jon L. *Poverty Point: A culture of the lower Mississippi Valley.* Baton Rouge: Louisiana Archaeological Survey and Antiquities Commission, Anthropological Study nr. 7, 1985.

Gimbutas, Marija. *Gods and Goddesses of Old Europe: 7000-3500 BC.* London: Thames and Hudson, 1974.

Glob, Peter Vilhelm. *Denmark: An archaeological history from the Stone Age to the Vikings.* Ithaca: Cornell University Press, 1971.

Goddard, Ives. "Eastern Algonquian Languages." *Handbook of the North American Indians.* Vol. 15: *Northeast.* Washington: Smithsonian Institution, 1978, pp. 70-77.

Griffin, James B. "Late Prehistory of the Ohio Valley." *Handbook of North American Indians.* Vol. 15: *Northeast.* Washington: Smithsonian Insitution, 1978, pp. 547-559.

_____. "The Northeast Woodlands Area." *Prehistoric Man in the New World.* Edited by Jesse D. Jennings and Edward Norbeck. Chicago: University of Chicago Press, 1964, pp. 223-258.

_____. "Prehistoric Settlement Patterns in the Northern Mississippi Valley and the Upper Great Lakes." *Prehistoric Settlement Patterns in the New World.* Edited by Gordon R. Willey. New York: Viking Fund, 1956, pp. 64-71.

Hallowell, A. Irving. "Northern Ojibwa Ecological Adaptation and Social Organization." *Contributions to Anthropology: Selected Papers of A. Irving Hallowell.* Chicago: University of Chicago Press, 1976, pp. 357-390.

_____. "Ojibwa Ontology, Behavior, and World View." *Contributions to Anthropology: Selected papers of A. Irving Hallowell.* Chicago: University of Chicago Press, 1976.

Hawkins, Gerald S. "Astroarchaeology: The unwritten evidence." *Archaeoastronomy in Pre-Columbian America.* Edited by Anthony F. Aveni. Austin: University of Texas Press, 1977, pp. 131-162.

Highwater, Jamake. *The Primal Mind.* New York: Harper & Row, 1981.

Horell, C. W. *et al. Land between the Rivers: The southern Illinois country.* Carbondale: Southern Illinois University Press, 1973.

Hudson, Travis and Underhay, Ernest. *Crystals in the Sky: An intellectual odyssey involving Chumash astronomy, cosmology, and rock art.* Ballena: Anthropological Papers X, 1978.

Hultkrantz, Åke. *Belief and Worship in Native North America.* Syracuse: Syracuse University Press, 1981.

_____. *Prairie and Plains Indians.* Leiden: E. J. Brill, 1973.

_____. *The Study of American Indian Religions.* New York: The Crossroad Publishing Company, 1983.

James, E. O. "Cremation and the Preservation of the Dead in North America." *American Anthropologist,* vol. XXX (1928). pp, 214-242.

Jennings, J. D. *Danger Cave.* Salt Lake City: University of Utah Press, 1957.

_____. *Prehistory of North America.* New York: McGraw-Hill Books, 1974, pp. 220-228.

_____. and Norbeck, Edward, eds. *Prehistoric Man in the New World.* Chicago: University of Chicago Press, 1964.

Kan, Michael and Wierzbowski, William. "Notes on an Important Southern Cheyenne Shield." *Native North American Art History: Selected readings.* Edited by Zena Pearlstone Mathews and Aldona Jonaitis. Palo Alto: Peek Publications, 1982, pp. 235-245.

Kehoe, Thomas and Kehoe, Alice B. "Stones, Solstices, and Sun Dance Structures," *Plains Anthropologist* 22 (1976), pp. 85-95.

Kisselgoff, Anna. "The Ancient Relationship of Goddesses and the Dance," *The New York Times,* December 14, 1986, section H, p. 18 ff.

Kohl, J. G. *Kitchi-Gami. Wanderings 'round Lake Superior.* London: Chapman and Hall, 1860.

Landis, Ruth. *Ojibwa Religion and the Midéwiwin.* Madison: University of Wisconsin Press, 1968.

Lauring, Palle. *Land of the Tollund Man: The prehistory and archaeology of Denmark.* New York: Macmillan, 1958.

Lévi-Strauss, Claude. *Myth and Meaning: Five talks for radio by Claude Lévi-Strauss.* Toronto: University of Toronto Press, 1978.

Lounsbury, Floyd G. "Iroquoian Languages." *Handbook of North American Indians.* Vol. 15: *Northeast.* Washington: Smithsonian Institution, 1978, pp. 334-343.

Lowie, Robert H. "Settlement and Dwellings of Plains Indians." *Native North American Art History: Selected readings.* Edited by Zena Pearlstone Mathews and Aldona Jonaitis. Palo Alto: Peek Publications, 1982, pp. 227-234.

Marriott, Alice. "The Trade Guild of the Southern Cheyenne Woman." *Native North American Art History: Selected readings.* Edited by Zena Pearlstone Mathews and Aldona Jonaitis. Palo Alto: Peek Publications, 1982, pp. 445-452.

Marschack, Alexander. *The Roots of Civilization: The cognitive beginnings of man's first art, symbol, and notation.* New York: McGraw Hill, 1972.

Martin, Calvin. "Subarctic Indians and Wildlife." *American Indian Environments: Ecological Issues in Native American History.* Edited by Christopher Vecsey and Robert W. Venables. Syracuse: Syracuse University, 1980, pp. 38-45.

Mason, Otis T. *Cradles of the American Aborigines: With notes on the artificial deformation of children among savages and civilized peoples.* Washington: Smithsonian, 1889.

Mathews, Zena Pearlstone. "Seneca Figurines: A case of misplaced modesty." *Native North American Art History: Selected readings.* Edited by Zena Pearlstone Mathews and Aldona Jonaitis. Palo Alto: Peek Publications, 1982, pp. 293-309.

Mayer, Dorothy. "An Examination of Miller's Hypothesis." *Native American Astronomy.* Edited by Anthony F. Aveni. Austin: University of Texas, 1975, pp. 180-201.

McCane-O'Connor, Mallory. "Prehistoric Ceramics: The Weeden Island tradition." *Native North American Art History: Selected readings.* Edited by Zena Pearlstone Mathews and Aldona Jonaitis. Palo Alto: Peek Publications, 1982, pp. 445-452.

Le megalithisme en midi-pyrenees: musée Saint-Raymond, Toulouse 21 mai-31 auot 1986. Toulouse: Société d'Exploitation de l'Imprimerie, 1986.

Morgan, John S. *When the Morning Stars Sang Together.* Agincourt: Book Society of Canada, 1974.

Morgan, William N. *Prehistoric Architecture in the Eastern United States.* Cambridge: The MIT Press, 1980.

Morrison, Joe. Interviewed by Peter Meggs, "Open House," CBC-FM, May 3, 1987.

Narr, Karl J. "Prehistoric Religion." *Encyclopaedia Britannica.* Vol. 14 (15th edition). Chicago: Encyclopaedia Britannica, 1984, pp. 984-989.

Neuman, Robert W. and Hawkins, Nancy W. *Louisiana Prehistory.* Baton Rouge: Louisiana Archaeological Survey and Antiquities Commission, Anthropological Study nr. 6, 1982.

Newall, R. S. *Stonehenge.* London: Her Majesty's Stationery Office, 1959.

Orchard, W. J. *The Stone Age on the Prairies.* Regina: School Aids and Text Book Publishing Co., 1942.

Otto, Martha. Personal communication, May 29, 1987. Ohio Historical Society, Columbus, Ohio.

Penney, David W. "The Adena Engraved Tablets: A study of art prehistory." *Native North American Art History: Selected readings.* Edited by Zena Pearlstone Mathews and Aldona Jonaitis. Palo Alto: Peek Publications, 1982, pp. 257-280.

_____. "Continuities of Imagery and Symbolism in the Art of the Woodlands." *Ancient Art of the American Woodland Indians.* David S. Brose, James W. Brown, David W. Penney. New York: Harry N. Abrams, 1985, pp. 147-198.

_____. "Introduction." *Ancient Art of the American Woodland Indians.* David S. Brose, James A. Brown, David W. Penney. New York: Harry N. Abrams, 1985, pp. 11-13.

_____. "The Late Archaic Period." *Ancient Art of the American Woodland Indians.* David S. Brose, James A. Brown, David W. Penney. New York: Harry N. Abrams, 1985, pp. 15-41.

Pfeiffer, John. "America's First City." *Horizon*, spring 1974, pp.59-63.

Pfeiffer, John E. *The Creative Explosion: An inquiry into the origins of art and religion.* New York: Harper & Row, 1982.

Phillips, Ruth. *Patterns of Power.* Kleinburg: McMichael Collection, 1984.

_____. Personal communication, May 26, 1987. Carleton University, Ottawa: Canadian Studies Institute.

Pocock, D. F. "North and South in the Book of Genesis." *Studies in Social Anthropology: Essays in memory of E. E. Evans-Pritchard by his former Oxford colleagues.* Edited by J. H. M. Beattie and R. G. Lienhardt. Oxford: Clarendon Press, 1975, pp. 273-284.

Reed, Erik. K. "Types of Village-Plan Layouts in the Southwest." *Prehistoric Settlement Patterns in the New World.* New York: Viking Fund, 1956, pp. 11-17.

Reed, Nelson A. "Monks and other Mississippian Mounds." *Explorations into Cahokia Archaeology.* Edited by Melvin L. Fowler. Illinois Archaeological Survey, Bulletin 7. Urbana: University of Illinois, 1973, pp. 31-42.

Ritchie, William A. "Prehistoric Settlement Patterns in Northeastern North America." *Prehistoric Settlement Patterns in the New World.* Edited by Gordon R. Willey. New York: Viking Fund, 1956, pp. 72-78.

Rolingson, Martha. Personal communication, May 29, 1987. Arkansas Archaeological Survey: Toltec Mounds State Park.

Safire, William. "On Language." *The New York Times Sunday Magazine,* May 17, 1987, p. 12.

Sanders, William T. and Marino, Joseph. *New World Prehistory.* Englewood Cliffs: Prentice-Hall, Inc., 1970.

Sapir, Edward. *Time Perspective in Aboriginal American Culture: A study in method.* Ottawa: Canada Department of Mines, Geological Survey, memoir 90, 1916.

Sears, William H. "The Southeastern United States." *Prehistoric Man in the New World.* Edited by Jesse David Jennings and Edward Norbeck. Chicago: University of Chicago Press, 1964, pp. 259-287.

Service, Elman R. *Profiles in Ethnology: A revision of A PROFILE OF PRIMITIVE CULTURE.* New York: Harper & Row, 1963.

Sherrod, P. Clay and Rolingson, Martha Ann. *Surveyors of the Ancient Mississippi Valley.* Fayetteville, Arkansas: Arkansas Archeological Survey Research Series, no. 28, 1987.

Shrum, E. "Meet the Mound Builders." *Hobbies,* June 1983, pp. 71-75.

Silverberg, Robert. *Mound Builders of Ancient America.* Greenwich: New York Graphic Society, 1968.

Smith, Harriet M. "The Murdock Mound: Cahokia Site." *Explorations into Cahokia Archaeology.* Edited by Melvin L. Fowler. Illinois Archaeological Society, Bulletin 7. Urbana: University of Illinois, 1973, pp. 49-80.

Spencer, R. F., Jennings, Jesse David, *et al. The Native Americans.* New York: Harper and Row, 1977.

Squier, E. G. and Davis, E. H. *Ancient Monuments of the Mississippi Valley: Comprising the results of the extensive original surveys and explorations.* Washington: Smithsonian Contributions to Knowledge, Vol. 1, 1848.

Starkloff, C. F. *The People of the Center: American Indian religion and Chrisitianity.* New York: Seabury Press, 1974.

Sullivan, W. "Ancient Mounds taken as Clues to Advanced Culture," *The New York Times*, June 19, 1979, p. C-3.

"Survey of Alberta may answer Questions about New World," *The Ottawa Citizen*, January 1, 1987, p. F-18.

Swadesh, Morris. "Linguistic Overview." *Prehistoric Man in the New World.* Edited by Jesse D. Jennings and Edward Norbeck. Chicago: University of Chicago Press, 1964.

Tanner, Adrian. *Bringing Home Animals: Religious ideology and mode of production of the Mistassini Cree hunters (*PhD dissertation, University of Toronto, 1976). Newfoundland: Memorial University Institute of Social and Economic Research, 1979.

Tooker, Elizabeth, ed. *Native North American Spirituality of the Eastern Woodlands: Sacred myths, dreams, visions, speeches, healing formulas, rituals, and ceremonials.* New York: Paulist Press, 1979.

Trigger, Bruce G. *The Huron: Farmers of the north.* New York: Holt, Rinehart, and Winston, 1969, pp. 102-120.

Tuck, James A. "Northern Iroquoian Prehistory." *Handbook of North American Indians.* Vol. 15: *Northeast.* Washington: Smithsonian Institution, 1978, pp. 322-333.

_____. "Regional Cultural Development, 3000-300 BC." *Handbook of North American Indians.* Vol. 15: *Northeast.* Washington: Smithsonian Institution, 1978, pp. 28-43.

Vastokas, Joan and Vastokas, Romas K. *Sacred Art of the Algonkians: A study of the Peterborough petroglyphs.* Peterborough: Mansard, 1973.

Vecsey, Christopher. "American Indian Environmental Religions." *American Indian Environment: Ecological issues in Native American history.* Edited by Christopher Vecsey and Robert W. Venables. Syracuse: Syracuse University Press, 1980, pp. 1-37.

_____. "Introduction." *Belief and Worship in Native North America.* Åke Hultkrantz. Syracuse: Syracuse University Press, 1981, pp. ix-xxvii.

_____. and Venables, Robert W., eds. *American Indian Environments: Ecological issues in Native American history.* Syracuse: Syracuse University Press, 1980.

Vogt, Evon Z. "An Appraisal of Prehistoric Settlement Patterns in the New World." *Prehistoric Settlement Patterns in the New World.* Edited by Gordon R. Willey. New York: Viking Fund, 1956, pp. 173-182.

Wainwright, Richard. *Prehistoric Remains in Britain,* Vol. 1. London: Constable, 1978.

Waugh, Earle H. and Prithipaul, K. Dad, eds. *Native Religious Traditions.* Waterloo: Canadian Corporation for Studies in Religion, 1979.

Webb, Clarence H. and Gregory, Hiram F. *The Caddo Indians of Louisiana.* Baton Rouge: Louisiana Archaeological Survey and Antiquities Commission, nr. 2, 1986.

Wedel, Waldo R. "Changing Settlement Patterns in the Great Plains." *Prehistoric Settlement Patterns in the New World.* Edited by Gordon R. Willey. New York: Viking Fund, 1956, pp. 81-92.

White, Randall. *Dark Caves, Bright Visions: Life in Ice Age Europe.* New York: American Museum of Natural History, 1986.

Wildschut, William. *Crow Indian Medicine Bundles.* New York: Heye Foundation, 1975.

Willey, Gordon R., ed. *Prehistoric Settlement Patterns in the New World.* New York: Viking Fund, 1956.

Williams, Stephen. "Settlement Patterns in the lower Mississippi Valley." *Prehistoric Settlement Patterns in the New World.* Edited by Gordon R. Willey. New York: Viking Fund, 1956, pp. 52-62.

Wittry, Warren L. "An American Woodhenge." *Native North American Art History: Selected readings.* Edited by Lena Pearlstone Mathews and Aldona Jonaitis. Palo Alto: Peek Publications, 1982, pp. 453-457.

Yarrow, H. C. *A Futher Contribution to the Study of Mortuary Customs of the North American Indian.* Washington: Bureau of Ethnology, First Annual Report, 1881.

_____. *Introduction to the Study of Mortuary Customs of the North American Indians.* Washington: Bureau of Ethnology, 1880.

Young, D. "The Secret City." *Chicago Tribune Magazine,* June 13, 1976, pp. 18 ff.

NATIVE AMERICAN STUDIES